Australian Education Review N

CONTINUING PROFESSIONAL EDUCATION

Promise and Performance

Edited by
Barrie Brennan

First published 1990
by The Australian Council for Educational Research Ltd
Radford House, Frederick Street, Hawthorn, Victoria 3122, Australia

Copyright © 1990 Australian Council for Educational Research

All rights reserved. Except as provided for by Australian copyright law, no part of this book may be reproduced without written permission from the publisher.

Cover by George Petrou Design
Edited by Jan Anderson

Printed by Brown Prior Anderson Pty Ltd

National Library of Australia
Cataloguing-in-Publication data:

Continuing professional education.

ISBN 0 86431 056 0.

1. Professional education — Australia. 2. Continuing education — Australia. 3. Career development — Australia. I. Brennan, Barrie. II. Australian Council for Educational Research. (Series: Australian education review; no. 30).

378.0130994

Contents

List of Tables   iv

List of Figures   iv

Part One: Setting the Scene *Barrie Brennan*
1 Introduction   2
2 Exploring the Major Terms   6
3 A Framework for Discussing Continuing Professional Education   33

Part Two: CPE in Practice: The Professional Profiles
4 The Legal Profession *John Nelson*   52
5 The Accounting Profession *Daljit Singh*   67
6 The Engineering Profession *Cyril Streatfield*   83
7 The Profession of Occupational Therapy *Gwynnyth Llewellyn*   97
8 The School Teaching Profession *Glyn France*   109

Part Three: Conclusion *Barrie Brennan*
9 Summary and Emerging Issues   126

Notes on Contributors   145

Tables

2.1	Employed Persons: Occupation of Full-Time and Part-Time Workers, November 1987	16
2.2	Employed Persons: Occupation and Status of Workers, November 1987	18
2.3	Employed Persons: Occupation, Age and Birthplace, November 1987	19
2.4	Employed Professionals in Minor Groups, November 1987	20
2.5	Public Esteem of Sixteen Occupations, Australia, 1977 and 1984	21
3.1	Data from CPE Survey, 1988	34
3.2	Trends in Mandatory CPE in the States of the USA for Twelve Professions, 1977–88	41
5.1	Summary of CPE Obligations for Members of the Australian Society of Accountants	71
5.2	Comparison of Acceptable CPE Activities — ASA and ICA	74
5.3	Comparison of CPE Revenues and Expenditures of the ASA and ICA, 1985 and 1987	79
8.1	Median Age of Classified Government School Teachers, Victoria, 1976 and 1985	110
8.2	Percentage Distributions of Government School Teachers by Length of Preservice Course, Australia, 1979	115

Figures

2.1	ASCO Minor Group 26: Social Professionals	14
2.2	Goal Orientations of Continuing Professional Education	31
6.1	The Main Elements of the National System for Engineers	91

Part One
SETTING THE SCENE

1
Introduction

BARRIE BRENNAN

What is continuing professional education, or 'CPE'? Put simply, it is the training of professionals after their initial, preservice training and induction or licensing into professional practice. However, the term CPE is not universally used. Specific terms are used in some professions to refer to the same type of activity; lawyers speak of continuing legal education (CLE); doctors of continuing medical education (CME); and engineers — simply of continuing education (CE). Rather than 'education' the word 'development' is sometimes used to describe inservice training. For example, accountants talk about professional development (PD). Generally speaking, the term CPE is favoured in North America and 'professional development' or 'continuing professional development' in the United Kingdom. The various terms, however, refer to essentially the same activity.

CPE is not a new phenomenon. Professionals have always tried to keep up-to-date with new techniques and developments in their field, often through informal study. However, there now appears to be an increased level of *organised* activity under the CPE 'banner'. Increasingly we see notices in professional newsletters and journals, as well as in the daily press, advertising what amounts to CPE activities. There are courses on computing for architects and veterinarians, seminars on understanding financial documents for engineers, workshops for doctors on dealing with patients from non-English-speaking backgrounds, and information days for teachers on their role in child-abuse cases. For professionals living in geographically remote areas, distance education programs — made possible by recent developments in communications technology — are becoming more common. Providers of CPE activities include professional organisations, higher education institutions, government instrumentalities and private consultants.

The Federal Government has recognised the importance of CPE by making special reference to the field in its discipline enquiries. National enquiries have already been conducted into the legal and engineering professions, and science and mathematics teachers are the subject of a current enquiry.

Because CPE is related to the initial preparation of professionals, changes as a result of the ministerial White Paper on Higher Education (Dawkins, 1988) are likely to raise the issue of how the new national system of higher education will deal with the pre- and inservice training of professionals.

Why has CPE come into prominence? The argument of this book is that CPE has become important because of the many changes in the context in which professionals practise in Australia. Factors such as the knowledge explosion, the introduction of new technologies, as well as changes in social and economic features of Australia, have impacted on the context in which professionals now practise. As a result, some of the traditional views about being a professional are being questioned. The reasons why CPE has become important in Australian professional life and the manner in which CPE is offered provide the justification for and structure of this book.

CPE activity is generally profession-specific, that is, teachers do their professional development, solicitors their CLE and physicians their CME. Also, research on CPE tends to be related to a specific profession. Hence, the references associated with the professional profiles herein are overwhelmingly drawn from the literature of the profession under discussion. There is not a great deal of cross-professional discussion or planning, though problems may be similar in closely related or quite unrelated professions. There has been no general across-professions enquiry or even survey of CPE in Australia, though such an enquiry was recommended by Johnson and Hinton (1986). This book therefore aims to redress the general lack of discussion of CPE across professions: general questions and issues that relate to professionals in all types of practice are raised.

CPE has become an important aspect of professional life in Australia because of significant changes in the context in which professionals practise. The objective of this book is to highlight the overall field of CPE, for all occupational groups that have gained or aspire to, the status of a profession, so that the potential of CPE to help professions meet the challenges of the changes in the context of professional life can be realised. It is the view of the writer that CPE can contribute to more effective professional practice in the changing Australian context.

Structure of the Book

The material in this book is organised into three main parts. Because changes in the context of professional practice are viewed as the major reason for the growing interest in CPE, Part One — as its title says — is devoted to 'Setting the Scene'. Following the present introduction, there is Chapter 2 — which examines the key terms from a number of perspectives so as to provide an overview of the context in which all professionals practise in Australia. Chapter 3 provides a broad framework for the discussion of CPE within any profession, features of an individual profession and factors in the management and provision of a CPE program. Such a 'framework' enables readers to examine CPE in their own or other professions.

Part Two is entitled 'CPE in Practice — The Professional Profiles'. It contains five professional profiles (Chapters 4 to 8 inclusive), written by persons involved in their own profession and its CPE. The five profiles were written during 1988. Subsequent developments affecting each profession mean that some of the details outlined in those chapters no longer apply. However, the key issues identified by the profiles are still relevant to the current debate about CPE within Australian professions. The profiles follow the framework outlined in Chapter 3, thus allowing for comparisons between the five professions. The professions chosen — law, accounting, engineering, occupational therapy and school teaching — are representative of professional life in Australia. They are five of the professional sub-groups in the *Australian Standard Classification of Occupations Dictionary* (Australian Bureau of Statistics & Department of Employment and Industrial Relations, 1987), an important document to consider when examining occupational groups in Australia. The five professions vary greatly in their nature and in the distance they have travelled down the 'CPE track'. Teachers are the largest professional group in Australia, whereas occupational therapists are a small, relatively new profession with a predominantly female membership. Engineers are not obliged to be registered to practise and have a professional organisation that was established by Royal Charter. Solicitors in New

South Wales have taken the initiative by making CPE mandatory for practitioners; one of the accountants' professional associations — the Australian Society of Accountants — has made very public its belief in CPE through the designation 'Certified Practising Accountant' (CPA), and the CPE requirements entailed. It should also be noted here that the specific problems of the school teaching profession and the differences between school teaching and the other professions discussed are reflected in the different approach in the school teaching profile (Chapter 8).

Part Three, which is synonymous with Chapter 9, is the 'Conclusion'. It seeks to draw a cross-professional picture of the stages of development that CPE has undergone so far in Australia. It raises important issues that are emerging for the field as a whole and suggests future directions for CPE in Australia.

A Note on Terminology

As mentioned in the opening paragraph of this chapter, the various professions use different terminology when referring to continuing professional education (CPE). Hence, although the authors of the five profiles (Chapters 4 to 8 inclusive) may at times refer simply to continuing professional education (CPE), they also use profession-specific terms, for example in the titles of their directors of CPE or in their policy documents. Rather than altering professions' terms to make them uniform, for example, changing the engineers' 'CE' to 'CPE', at the risk of introducing inaccuracies — it was decided to leave profiles basically as the authors had written them. As a result, profiles in some instances contain both the general term, CPE, and the one specific to the profession (CE, PD, etc.).

References

Australian Bureau of Statistics & Department of Employment and Industrial Relations. (1987). *Australian standard classification of occupations dictionary.* Canberra: Australian Government Publishing Service.

Dawkins, J. S. (1988). *Higher education: A policy statement.* ('Dawkins' White Paper.') Canberra: Australian Government Publishing Service.

Johnson, R. & Hinton, F. (1986). *It's human nature: Non-award adult and continuing education in Australia.* Canberra: Commonwealth Tertiary Education Commission.

2
Exploring the Major Terms

BARRIE BRENNAN

There are two sets of terms that must be defined at the outset. One set of terms revolves around the word 'profession' and its derivatives, 'professional' and 'professionalisation'. The other set of terms focuses on 'education', particularly 'continuing education'. This chapter explores these terms from a number of perspectives. While the historical dimension is important, current usage is stressed. Although examples of the definitions of the terms are cited from other nations, Australian uses are stressed. How other people in other places and at other times have used the major terms is relevant. However, the usage in contemporary Australia with its own social, political and economic context and all the idiosyncrasies of this context is the central focus.

The exploration is not an historical analysis, a sociological treatise, or an examination of case histories to derive legalistic interpretations of the terms. All these approaches have merit, and provide insight into the meanings of the terms. However, one of the objectives of the exploration is to suggest that the terms that are central to this volume are used in different ways by different groups and agencies and that different emphases are placed on varying dimensions of the terms by different users.

While a definitive statement about the central terms of this book — those related to 'profession' and 'education' — may be deemed to be desirable, such an objective may result in a restricted, or even unreal, description of CPE in Australia.

Exploring perspectives on the term 'profession'

Lists of Characteristics

A common response to the question of defining and explaining the term 'profession' is to list the key characteristics of a profession. Two frequently cited lists of characteristics of a profession are reproduced. One is a brief list of propositions, whereas the other is a more detailed explanation.

The American Association of Professors of Higher Education (1975, p. 5) concluded that a profession incorporates the following seven characteristics:

1 An organised body of intellectual theory constantly expanded by research.
2 An intellectual technique.
3 A close-knit association of members with a high quality of communication between them.
4 A period of long training.
5 A series of standards and an enforced statement of ethics.
6 Applications to the practical affairs of man.
7 Active influence on public policy in its field.

Schein (1972, pp. 8–9) has proposed ten characteristics based on the traditional or learned professions:

1 The professional, as distinct from the amateur, is engaged in a full-time occupation that comprises his principal source of income.
2 The professional is assumed to have a strong motivation or calling as a basis for his choice of a professional career and is assumed to have a stable lifetime commitment to that career.
3 The professional possesses a specialised body of knowledge and skills that are acquired during a prolonged period of education and training.
4 The professional makes his decisions on behalf of a client in terms of general principles, theories, or propositions, which he applies to the particular case under consideration,...
5 ...the professional is assumed to have a service orientation, which means that he uses his expertise on behalf of the particular needs of his client. This service implies diagnostic skill, competent application of general knowledge to the special needs of the client, and an absence of self-interest.
6 The professional's service to the client is assumed to be based on the objective needs of the client and independent of the particular

sentiments that the professional may have about the client. The professional promises a 'detached' diagnosis. The client is expected to be fully frank in revealing potentially unlikeable things about himself; the professional as his part of the contract is expected to withhold moral judgement, no matter how he may feel personally about the client's revelation. Thus, the professional relationship rests on a kind of mutual trust between the professional and client.

7   The professional is assumed to know better what is good for the client than the client himself. In other words, the professional demands autonomy of judgement of his own performance. Even if the client is not satisfied, the professional will, in principle, permit only his colleagues to judge his performance. Because of this demand for this professional autonomy, the client is in a potentially vulnerable position. How does he know whether he has been cheated or harmed? The profession deals with this potential vulnerability by developing strong ethical and professional standards for its members. Such standards may be expressed as codes of conduct and are usually enforced by colleagues through professional associations or through licensing examinations designed and administered by fellow professionals.

8   Professionals form professional associations which define criteria of admission, educational standards, licensing or other formal entry examinations, career lines within the profession, and areas of jurisdiction for the profession. Ultimately, the professional association's function is to protect the autonomy of the profession; it develops reasonably strong forms of self-government by setting rules or standards for the profession.

9   Professions have great power and status in the area of their expertise, but their knowledge is assumed to be specific. A professional does not have a license to be a 'wise man' outside the area defined by his training.

10 Professionals make their service available but ordinarily are not allowed to advertise or to seek out clients. Clients are expected to initiate the contract and then accept the advice and service recommended, without appeal to outside authority.

While the approach to defining profession by means of a list of characteristics or criteria may have some general descriptive or comparative uses, problems remain. Such problems are illustrated by the lack of consensus in the literature concerning the list of characteristics, either the number of items and/or their content. The various lists tend to be writer-specific. For example, Jarvis (1983) notes that some 25 writers on the professions had developed 23 different lists of characteristics of a profession. When examining these various lists, it is difficult to estimate the significance of either adding or subtracting individual characteristics. Further, the lists of characteristics tend to be dominated by the features of the traditional professions. They incorporate features that have been long recognised and accepted. As a result they can be criticised as setting up an ideal that may have been possible in the past but may only be marginally relevant in the present or the future. The danger is that new or emerging factors shaping professional work may be overlooked or given a very low priority in the extant lists of characteristics. Another problem they generate is the temptation to apply them universally. Social, cultural, or economic factors that are specific to a nation such as Australia may have a significant role in defining the characteristics of the professions as a whole or to single or groups of professions and yet not be captured by any one list of characteristics.

Professionalisation

This derivative of 'profession' has been used by Houle (1980) to describe a process. The process, he argued, acts at two levels: the degree to which a particular occupational group has reached professional status or the means by which established professions seek to preserve and strengthen their professional status.

Because of Houle's significance as a writer on the professions and continuing professional education, the reproduction of his list of the characteristics of dynamic professionalisation is warranted (Houle, 1980, pp. 35–73). The characteristics are arranged under three headings that relate to the three types of characteristics — conceptual, performance and collective identity characteristics.

Conceptual characteristics
1 Clarification of the profession's changing functions (mission) — by as many members of the profession as possible.

Performance characteristics
2 Mastery of theoretical knowledge.
3 Capacity to solve problems.
4 Use of practical knowledge.
5 Self-enhancement.

Collective identity characteristics
6 Formal training.
7 Credentialing.
8 Creation of a sub-culture.
9 Legal reinforcement.
10 Public acceptance.
11 Ethical practice.
12 Penalties.

13 Relations to other vocations.
14 Relations to users of service.

Houle has claimed that his concept of professionalisation is 'dynamic', in that it recognises the importance of changes in the characteristics. For example, there is a need to define and redefine the profession's mission (Characteristic 1), re-examine as an ongoing activity relations with other vocations (Characteristic 13) and users (Characteristic 14). In this respect, Houle's conceptualisation overcomes a problem with other lists such as that of Schein — that they can be assumed to be static and unconcerned with changes within professions or in the context in which professional life is practised.

However, Houle's professionalisation does share with other lists of professional characteristics the problem of being idealistic, in the sense of describing a process that will result in the profession becoming better, potentially improving its performance in all the characteristics. Woll (1984) has criticised Houle's professionalisation process on this very point. The professionalisation process will not inevitably or naturally result in a better profession. Woll uses the concept of control to illustrate his criticism. In the professionalisation process, sub-groups within the profession with a particular political or philosophical point of view may seek to gain control of the profession. The mission can be subverted. Those not following a particular official line may be punished. There is no inevitability of betterness, argues Woll, in professionalisation.

While Woll's criticism is focused on Houle's conceptualisation, there have been others who have been highly critical of the role of professionals and the impact of professionalisation. Taking the broad socio-political point of view, the argument is advanced, in complete contrast to Houle, that not only is professionalisation a 'bad thing' but that the situation will become worse rather than better. In *The Disabling Professions*, Illich, for example, has focused on the negative view of professions and professionalisation through the concept of power, arguing that professionals can be compared to racketeers and gangsters, but that the professions are more harmful:

> Let us face the fact that the bodies of specialists that now dominate the creation, adjudication and implementation of needs are a new kind of cartel. They are more deeply entrenched than a Byzantine bureaucracy, more international than a world church, more stable than any labour union, endowed with wider competencies than any other shaman, and

equipped with a tighter hold over those they claim as victims than any mafia.

The new organised specialists must, though, be carefully distinguished from racketeers. Educators, for instance, now tell society what must be learned, and are in a position to write off as valueless what has been learned outside of school. By establishing this kind of monopoly that enables them to preclude you from shopping elsewhere and from making your own booze, they at first seem to fit the dictionary definition of gangsters. But gangsters, for their own profit, corner a basic necessity by controlling supplies. Today, doctors and social workers — as formerly only priests and jurists — gain legal power to create the need that, by law, they alone will be allowed to satisfy. (Illich, 1977, pp. 15–16)

The problem of who controls the professionalisation process has been raised by Woll: Illich has painted an extreme picture of the effects of the process. Professionalisation will not necessarily result in better professions, or a better society.

The development of lists of characteristics to describe professions provides a useful, but limited, perspective from which to view professional practice in contemporary Australia. The concept of professionalisation provides a more useful description because of the recognition of the reaction of professions to change. Questions have been raised above, however, in relation to the possible results of the process of professionalisation and to the importance of who controls the process that responds to change within a profession.

The following section discusses a very different perspective on the professions. Unlike the optimism of Houle and the pessimism of Illich, the labour-market perspective on the professions is comparative and objective.

Labour-market Approach

In Australia, as in other developed Western nations, governments, and their bureaucracies, have become increasingly involved in definitional and other questions associated with the professions. Part of the reason for this involvement derives from the large financial contribution governments often make to the preservice training of professionals through the higher education sector. Also important is the increasing role of governments in economic planning and labour-market needs, of which the professions form a significant part. An example of government involvement is provided by the recent publication in Australia, after almost a decade of planning and testing, of the first *Australian Standard*

Classification of Occupations Dictionary (Australian Bureau of Statistics & Department of Employment and Industrial Relations, 1987) — which shall be referred to as 'the Dictionary' or 'ASCO' hereinafter. From the evidence presented in the introduction to the Dictionary, professionals and professional associations were not specifically consulted in the planning and testing process — unless they have been classified under the heading of 'users'.

The conceptual basis of the classification of occupations contained in the ASCO document is one of skill, with two important sub-classifications, namely skills level and skill specification. Three variables are used in the measurement of skill level: formal training; on-the-job training; and previous experience. Skill specification is a function of the field of knowledge required, tools or equipment required, material worked on, and goods and services produced.

The occupational classification is organised on the basis of eight major groups of occupations and a number of minor groups within each major group. The major groups are:

- managers and administrators;
- professionals;
- para-professionals;
- tradespersons;
- clerks;
- salespersons and personal service workers;
- plant and machine operators and drivers; and
- labourers and related workers.

Professionals are defined by ASCO as people who perform analytical, conceptual and creative duties requiring a high level of intellectual ability and a thorough understanding of an extensive body of theoretical knowledge. Most occupations in this major group have a level of skills commensurate with a three- or four-year degree or diploma, with some occupations requiring a longer basic degree and/or postgraduate qualifications.

According to ASCO, duties performed by professionals include:

conducting and analysing research to extend the body of knowledge in their discipline; developing techniques to apply this knowledge; designing products, physical structures and engineering systems; identifying and treating, or advising on, health, social and personal problems; teaching the theory and practice of one or more disciplines; developing and coordinating administrative programs; and communicating ideas through language and artistic media (including visual and performing arts). (Australian Bureau of Statistics & Department of Employment and Industrial Relations, 1987, p. 37)

The nine major occupational sub-groups within the ASCO professional category are:

- natural scientists;
- building professionals and engineers;
- health diagnosis and treatment practitioners;
- school teachers;
- other teachers and instructors;
- social professionals;
- business professionals;
- artists and related professionals; and
- miscellaneous professionals.

For each of these sub-groups ASCO provides a description of the skill levels, duties and constituent occupations. Figure 2.1 reproduces ASCO material relating to one of the professional sub-groups, social professionals. Social professionals provide guidance to clients or members of a congregation in social, educational, vocational, legal and spiritual matters, to enable them to find and use resources to overcome difficulties and achieve goals. ASCO, with its discussion of all occupations, its emphasis on 'skill', and its major reference point as the labour market, provides different emphases from the lists of characteristics.

The overall allocation of occupations within the major and minor categories provides insights into the way some of the traditionally held beliefs about professions are viewed from a labour-market perspective. For example, the first major category is not professionals, but managers and administrators. Managers take pride of place. In the legal 'profession', judges are classified as managers, while lawyers are in the professional category. Similarly, school teachers are classified as professionals but principals are classified as managers. The pre-eminence of professionals is not recognised by ASCO. The classification also illustrates that there is the potential for disunity in professional organisations because of the differing roles of those members who have become managers and administrators.

The ASCO approach includes physiotherapists and occupational therapists in the same professional group as medical practitioners, the

Skill level
Occupations in this minor group have a level of skill commensurate with a three- or four-year degree or diploma.

Duties
Include discussing, analysing and assessing the legal, social or spiritual needs of individuals, groups or committees, advising individuals or groups of their rights and obligations and on possible courses of action; representing or supporting individuals or groups undergoing difficulties; performing ceremonies and preparing documents in connection with social, spiritual and legal matters or important personal events; maintaining records and writing reports.

Content

2601	**SOCIAL WORKERS**
2601–11	Social Planner and Administrator
2601–13	Community Social Worker
2601–15	Social Case Worker
2603	**COUNSELLORS**
2603–11	Rehabilitation Counsellor
2603–13	Marriage Counsellor
2603–15	Family Court Counsellor
2603–17	Careers Counsellor and Adviser
2603–99	Counsellors
2605	**LAWYERS**
2605–11	Barristers
2605–13	Solicitor
2605–91	Articled Clerk
2605–99	Lawyers
2607	**MINISTERS OF RELIGION**
2607–11	Minister of Religion

Figure 2.1 Minor Group: Social Professionals

Source: *Dictionary of the Australian Standard Classification of Occupations*, 1987, p. 90.

health diagnosis and treatment practitioners. Also included here are chiropractors and osteopaths — practitioners who may not be accepted by many members of the medical establishment as being 'professional'. Omitted from this particular group are nurses who are categorised as para-professionals, despite their training and level of skill.

The grouping of professional occupations in the minor categories suggests skill areas that may have not received attention in other discussions on the occupations and may be becoming important as considerations. For example, lawyers are in the minor group of social professionals with counsellors, social workers and ministers of religion, while accountants are categorised as business professionals with computer professionals and public relations officers. There are implications for preservice training, and CPE, from the interpretation of the law as a social profession.

The labour-market approach, as evidenced in Australia by ASCO, provides a different perspective on the professions. They are not 'separate' but are considered to be just part of the labour force. Nor are the professions given pre-eminence. The labour-market approach has implications for professional organisations in areas such as preservice training and the boundaries between professional and non-professional occupations' special areas of competence. The labour-market approach recognises the importance of CPE because of its emphasis on *on-the-job* training.

Demographic Features

An examination of the demographic features of Australia's professionals provides a quantitative measure of the size of the task being addressed in this book. Data from the *Labour Force Reports* of the Australian Bureau of Statistics are particularly useful because they have been analysed according to the categories of ASCO discussed above.

Table 2.1 shows that in November 1987 full- and part-time workers totalled 7,160,000 persons. Of this total 867,500 (12.1 per cent) were classified as professionals by ASCO. Therefore, approximately one in eight of the workforce are professionals, while one in ten are managers or administrators and one in sixteen are para-professionals. The target group for CPE is thus large. Social changes in recent times have focused on the role and status of women, particularly in relation to the workforce. Table 2.1 indicates that the participation of women in the professional category overall is 40 per cent, the same percentage as for the labour force as a whole. The data also indicate that 58 per cent of women working as professionals are married. The sex ratio in a profession and particularly the involvement of married women has important implications for the programming of CPE. Consideration needs to be given to the timing,

Table 2.1 Employed Persons: Occupation of Full-Time and Part-Time Workers, November 1987 ('000s)

Occupation major group	Full-time workers		Part-time workers			Females			Total persons
	Males	Females	Males	Females	Total males	Married	Total		
Managers and administrators	588.3	130.1	16.4	45.5	604.7	139.0	175.6		780.3
Professionals	485.7	253.1	35.1	93.7	520.8	203.2	346.7		867.5
Para-professionals	229.5	125.0	9.0	66.2	238.4	112.5	191.2		429.6
Tradespersons	970.8	73.1	38.4	37.2	1009.2	59.8	110.4		1119.6
Clerks	276.5	608.9	14.5	301.0	290.9	553.9	909.9		1200.8
Salespersons and personal service workers	317.5	299.6	66.6	354.1	384.1	326.5	653.7		1037.8
Plant and machine operators, and drivers	466.1	77.0	22.9	20.3	489.0	69.6	97.3		586.3
Labourers and related workers	626.6	177.9	113.4	220.1	740.1	273.5	397.9		1138.0
Total	3960.9	1744.7	316.3	1138.0	4277.2	1737.9	2882.7		7159.9

Source: *The Labour Force, Australia*, Australian Bureau of Statistics, November 1987, p. 34.

length and location of activities as the need arises for women's career development to relate to periods of child bearing and rearing.

One of the assumptions about being a professional in traditional occupations was that the practitioner was an independent operator. Data in Table 2.2 (page 18) indicate that in Australia, at least for the ASCO professional group, such an assumption is no longer valid. Only 5.3 per cent of professionals are employers, a similar proportion are self-employed, and almost 90 per cent are wage or salary earners. Even after excluding the largest single group of professionals, school teachers, of whom all are salary earners, only 7.5 and 7.6 per cent of the remainder are employers and self-employed respectively. The data clearly show that assumptions in the Schein list about autonomous professionals must be questioned in Australia where 90 per cent of professionals are employees. The apparent widespread growth of the employment of professionals in the government and private sectors has important implications for professionals as a whole and for their CPE in particular.

Age profiles are important for labour-market planners. They can also be important for CPE planners. The professional category, according to the labour-force data, is not concentrated in the older age cohorts. Almost two out of every three persons in the professional group are in the 25–44 age group, as shown in Table 2.3 (page 19), compared to a little more than half of the total workforce. This table also gives data on the birthplace of employed persons: for the professional group 25.7 per cent, or just more than one in four were born in a country other than Australia, a figure similar to that of the workforce as a whole. The data indicate that in any particular profession there may be an important sub-population for CPE activities. The data also raise the question for CPE planning and provision of the acceptance of overseas qualifications for professional practice in Australia.

Until the 1986 Census data are processed, recent information on the members of those in specific professions is not available. However, national data on the ASCO minor groups are shown in Table 2.4 (page 20). Data for the major group, professionals, are reproduced, together with the numbers in the minor groups within the category and the participation of women in each grouping of professions. School teachers are the largest professional group, followed by business professionals, building professionals and engineers, and health diagnosis and treatment practitioners. As far as female participation is concerned, the highest levels are indicated in the school teacher and miscellaneous groups, while

Table 2.2 Employed Persons: Occupation and Status of Workers, November 1987 ('000s)

Occupation major group	Employers		Self-employed		Wage & salary earners		Total[a]		
	Males	Females	Males	Females	Males	Females	Males	Females	Persons
Managers and administrators	97.5	35.3	163.5	71.9	340.3	65.5	604.7	175.6	780.3
Professionals	39.4	6.7	26.5	20.1	454.5	319.5	520.8	346.7	867.5
Para-professionals	4.2	b	9.4	b	224.9	189.3	238.4	191.2	429.6
Tradespersons	57.8	6.6	137.3	14.4	812.4	88.6	1009.2	110.4	1119.6
Clerks	b	31.4	b	35.1	286.5	824.5	290.9	909.9	1200.8
Salespersons and personal service workers	15.8	21.3	36.7	47.7	327.2	576.7	384.1	653.7	1037.8
Plant and machine operators, and drivers	13.3	b	52.4	5.4	421.8	90.6	489.0	97.3	586.3
Labourers and related workers	11.8	4.2	49.0	17.0	664.3	364.9	740.1	397.9	1138.0
Total	240.1	107.0	477.3	213.4	3531.9	2519.5	4277.2	2882.7	7159.9

Notes: a Includes unpaid family helpers.
       b Numbers are too small to be included because of the standard error involved.

Source: *The Labour Force, Australia*, Australian Bureau of Statistics, November 1987, p. 34.

Table 2.3 Employed Persons: Occupation, Age and Birthplace, November 1987 ('000s)

Occupation major group	Age group						Total	Born in Australia	Born outside Australia
	15–19	20–24	25–34	35–44	45–54	55 and over			
Managers and administrators	4.4	25.9	158.3	255.7	183.7	152.3	780.3	604.4	175.9
Professionals	6.7	81.4	299.5	267.7	137.4	74.8	867.5	644.5	223.0
Para-professionals	15.3	55.0	149.1	114.2	65.4	30.7	429.6	327.3	102.3
Tradespersons	122.2	191.6	312.8	243.8	153.8	95.5	1119.6	796.7	322.9
Clerks	92.8	216.6	355.8	302.4	158.3	74.9	1200.8	943.1	257.7
Salespersons and personal service workers	235.0	175.3	247.8	213.4	109.3	57.0	1037.8	828.0	209.8
Plant and machine operators, and drivers	19.0	63.4	159.2	171.0	112.0	61.7	586.3	391.7	194.6
Labourers and related workers	157.4	151.7	261.8	251.7	196.4	119.0	1138.0	813.1	324.9
Total	652.9	960.8	1944.1	1819.9	1116.4	665.8	7159.9	5348.8	1811.1

Source: *The Labour Force, Australia*, Australian Bureau of Statistics, November 1987, p. 34.

Table 2.4 Employed Professionals in Minor Groups, November 1987 ('000s)

Professional minor groups	Males	Females Married	Total	Persons
Natural scientists	26.0	4.3	8.2	34.2
Building professionals and engineers	98.6	(a)	(a)	102.5
Health diagnosis and treatment practitioners	50.1	20.8	32.5	82.6
School teachers	86.2	102.3	164.0	250.2
Other teachers and instructors	46.3	23.7	36.5	82.8
Social professionals	36.3	6.6	16.2	52.6
Business professionals	125.4	23.5	44.6	170.0
Artists and related professionals	35.4	9.6	21.4	56.8
Miscellaneous professionals	16.4	11.2	19.4	35.7

Note: (a) Numbers are too small to be included because of the standard error involved.

Source: *The Labour Force, Australia,* Australian Bureau of Statistics, November 1987, p. 36.

participation in the building professionals and engineers group is very low.

The national demographic data for professional groups, as defined by ASCO, suggest some important issues for consideration by those concerned with professional education, professional associations and CPE. For those concerned with the management and provision of CPE in a particular profession, demographic data are important for defining general policy and specific programs for target groups. For all those involved in professional associations, and particularly in CPE, demographic information is a reminder that it is vital to know the composition of the membership of a profession.

Client Perceptions

In five of Schein's characteristics of a professional, the client is mentioned. How are Australian professionals perceived by their clients or the users, real or potential, of professional services? While individual

Table 2.5 Public Esteem of Sixteen Occupations, Australia, 1977 and 1984 (per cent)

Occupation	June 1977	Feb. 1984	Variation
Physician	70	63	-7
Lawyer	40	45	+5
Clergyman	47	44	-3
Chemist	36	39	+3
Engineer	35	37	+2
University professor	31	36	+5
High school teacher	44	36	-8
Primary school teacher	41	34	-7
Industrialist, private business	28	33	+5
Officer in armed forces	17	25	+8
Ambassador, diplomat	18	22	+4
Nuclear physicist	16	18	+2
Company executive	12	18	+6
Politician	15	16	+1
Newspaper editor	13	16	+3
Bookshop owner	5	9	+4
None, Don't know	10	2	-8

Source: Australian Public Opinion Polls (The Gallup Method). Reproduced courtesy of *The Herald*, Melbourne.

clients have their own relationships with the professionals with whom they deal, what views are held about professions as a whole or one profession in comparison with others? One source of data is public opinion polls. Australian Public Opinion Polls (the Gallup Method) reports the results of their 1977 and 1984 surveys which asked respondents to select five occupations, from a list of sixteen, which had the greatest esteem in their view. The data, shown in Table 2.5, reveal that clients of professions view various professions with different degrees of esteem. In addition, this level of esteem may vary from time to time.

While the relevance of popular esteem for an individual profession or the significance of public opinion polls can be questioned, what cannot be questioned is that the attitudes of the community, the clients of the services of professionals, are a significant factor for professional practice as part of the context of professional practice. Further, attitudes towards professionals, as with all attitudes, change over time. The range of attitudes held by the community towards professions as a whole, or individual professions, cannot be summarily dismissed.

Whereas esteem was the criterion used in the Gallup Poll method to rank professions, Daniel's study investigated power, privilege and prestige in relation to occupations in Australia (Daniel, 1983). She asked respondents to rate the status of over 150 occupations on a seven-point scale. Medicine, law, academia, the church and the officer corps maintained their dominance as the most highly rated professions, followed by the professions of architect, dentist, engineer, veterinary surgeon, accountant, surveyor and orchestra conductor. The ratings confirm the link between power and privilege in society's consciousness of prestige. Daniel notes that the prestige of the two leading professions (medicine and the law) has been maintained despite criticism by consumers or client groups.

Professions are the most highly rated occupations in Australian society from the point of view of esteem and prestige. The fears of Illich (1977, pp. 14–15), quoted above, do not seem to have influenced the views of the Australian clients of the services of professionals, and the Australian com-munity's perception of professionals is one of high esteem, power, prestige and privilege. However, the particular or relative standing of a profession may vary from time to time.

Reviewing Perspectives on 'Profession'

The Schein characteristics will be 'revisited' with twin objectives. They will be used as the basis for summarising significant material presented in the previous four sections and, in addition, to draw some tentative conclusions about the way profession and professional are operationally defined in contemporary Australia.

Schein's first characteristic emphasises the comparison with 'amateur' and stresses the term 'income'. The labour-market approach suggests that professional occupations should be discussed in relation to other major groups — managers and administrators, and para-professionals — rather than in relation to the general term 'amateur'. The labour-market perspective stresses the notion that professions cannot be considered alone but rather that they must be considered in relation to the workforce as a whole.

The emphasis on income suggests that professionals are self-employed. The Australian Bureau of Statistics data indicate that almost 90 per cent of professionals in Australia are employees, receiving a salary.

The second Schein characteristic places emphasis on commitment. In relation to commitment, the point should be made that in this characteristic, as in them all, there is the use of the male pronoun, and, it can be assumed, concern about the male perspective. In relation to commitment to a career for example, the female orientation is potentially very different from that of the male. Since the demographic data reveals different levels of female participation in various professions, females' perception of commitment should not be assumed to be the same as that of males.

While data was not presented on the frequency of people changing professions, the division in the ASCO classification between managers and administrators, and professionals highlights the dilemma faced by many professionals with respect to their commitment to a career and a profession. The teacher becomes a principal; the engineer becomes a construction manager. Does the principal identify with a new profession of educational administrator; is the engineer now a neophyte manager? To what profession and professional body are these persons now committed? In a few instances professionals partly solve such problems by becoming members of two professional associations. An engineer working, say, as a management consultant may belong to both the Institution of Engineers, Australia and the Institute of Management Consultants in Australia.

The third characteristic emphasises knowledge and skills gained in training. The impossibility of including all the knowledge and skills required for the professional in his or her practice is now acknowledged. The possibility of initial training being progressively extended to cope with this problem is being seen as an inadequate solution and has been recognised as a non-possibility in the ministerial Green Paper (Dawkins, 1987.) The importance of updating knowledge and skill is also accepted.

There are other changes that cause the third Schein characteristic to be questioned. Knowledge is expanding and changing rapidly in professional areas. As a result there are two parallel developments. Increased specialisation is occurring at the same time as the development of a 'team' approach to professional work. Both developments call into question the assertion of 'a' body of knowledge as claimed by Schein.

Characteristics 4–7 developed by Schein emphasise the relationship with the client. While the data presented on the esteem and prestige of the professions indicates that the clients of professional services overall rate the professionals highly, there are developments in Australian society that suggest changes in the relationship and changes in the way professions are perceived. Schein describes the relationship in terms of 'detachment' and 'trust'. However, Partlett (1985, p. vii) notes:

> [the] liability of professionals has grown apace in the past 15 years. The signs are bountiful that the recent acceleration in the law will continue into the future. It is argued that increasing exposure of professionals to liability can be seen as a more general movement in holding professions accountable for their actions.

The notions that professionals are still held in high esteem by the community and that they are also expected to be accountable are not incompatible. The professional–client relationship is changing. From one of simple trust, or fear or awe, the relationship is becoming one of a legal and commercial nature. If a client's high level of expectation of the professional's service is not attained, then the client may have recourse to the law. Schein's assertion that if the client is not satisfied with the professional's service the professional will 'permit only his colleagues to judge his performance' (Characteristic 7) is no longer tenable. The ASCO minor group classifications reflect some recognition of the changed professional–client relationship. Members of the legal profession are described as 'social professionals', that is, they are in the same category as ministers of religion and counsellors. Perhaps more emphasis should be given to the degree of direct social contact professionals have with their clients.

In contemporary Australia there are changes in the relationship between the professional and the client. These changes bring into question claims in some of Schein's characteristics. The changes, however, place greater emphasis on aspects of other characteristics.

Characteristics 7 and 8 stress the role of the professional association. In the changing professional–client relationship the importance of the association's codes of conduct (Characteristic 7) increases. Schein also notes the importance of the professional association enforcing codes of conduct. However, in relation to the enforcement of standards of conduct and licensing, the data presented suggest that the situation in Australia today may not be as simple as Schein suggests.

The possibility of the control of professional associations was raised under the heading of professionalisation. Within the professional association there is the possibility of pressure being exerted on the incompetent practitioner or the member whose views are different from those in control. While there are arguments for and against what Schein has called the 'autonomy' of professions being protected by the association (Characteristic 8), the question 'do professional associations have the degree of autonomy that Schein claims?' must be asked. If the client has recourse to the courts, if governments are involved in initial training, registration and re-registration, if economists are concerned with the overall contribution of professions within a labour-market conception of the workforce, can the professional association maintain the autonomy claimed by Schein?

Characteristic 9 refers to the specific knowledge of a professional. As knowledge has developed, there has been increased specialisation. How does the professional association cope with the proliferation of specialisations within its membership? How does the association protect the boundaries of its professional area of expertise? Two examples illustrate these changes and dilemmas. As libraries become filled with computer technology, does the profession of librarian become just a specialisation within the larger profession of computer professionals? With specialisation the team approach has developed. In the field of sport, what are the boundaries between the specialised knowledge of the doctor, psychologist, chiropractor, physiotherapist and fitness conditioner?

Finally, Schein's tenth characteristic notes that the professional does not advertise. Limited advertising for a number of professions is now allowed in Australia. However, what is significant is that the context of professional practice in Australia has changed from the social and economic environment in which the Schein list of characteristics may have been applicable. Professionals need to be more competitive with one another and with other professions to attract clients. In some instances they even need to be able to compete with their clients' abilities; to wit private individuals doing their own conveyancing with 'do-it-yourself' kits rather than using a solicitor. The relationship with clients has changed. From an interpersonal relationship of trust, it has become a legal–commercial relationship, in which advertising has become an acceptable strategy.

The Schein list of characteristics has been shown to have less relevance to professional life in Australia than it may have had in the past. What then has the exploration of the key terms profession and professional, from a number of perspectives, revealed about the way these terms are operationally defined in contemporary Australia? There are many different professions and they make up a large and significant occupational group. Professionals have a long period of initial training. The training emphasises knowledge and skill. Both the knowledge and skill, because of limits on initial training and the expansion of knowledge, require up-dating during a professional career. The high esteem in which society holds professionals is matched by a high level of expectation with the result that professionals are increasingly required to be accountable. Such accountability is not restricted to fellow professionals through a professional association but to governments and clients, particularly through litigation. Thus, the professional association has a role not only in protecting the members against outside influence and other professions but also in enforcing standards and codes of behaviour among members. The question that is central, then, to this book is: 'What role has CPE in the life of professionals in contemporary Australia?'. While the relevance of CPE to some of the issues mentioned above may be obvious, the question remains as to what extent CPE may have a role in contributing to the wide range of issues confronting professions at this time?

Exploring the terms 'education' and 'continuing professional education'

Rather than examine the terms 'education' and 'CPE' from a number of different perspectives, as was the method with profession and professional, in this section two major approaches will be used. The first approach will be to examine the relationship between CPE and initial training and the second will examine the goals of CPE. The choice of this approach is partly based on the assumption that CPE can most simply be defined as post-initial training. Another justification for the approach is that CPE should, in the view of the author, be considered not as a separate entity but as part of the overall career of a professional and that CPE should have an influence on initial training rather than CPE being dependent on initial training. Further, if the policy of discipline reviews becomes a standard method of enquiry into professions, then the longitudinal view, covering preservice as well as inservice training, is likely to be adopted. Finally, the approach is justified in terms of lifelong education. The justification for dealing with CPE through the goals of the activity is that the focus on goals allows for the discussion of the role of CPE in a wide context covering the types of questions and issues raised in connection with the discussion of professionalisation and the context of professional practice in Australia.

Initial Training and CPE

What appears to be clear is that professionals as a group have had a good deal of experience of education and have been among the most successful products of the educational system. They have completed primary and secondary levels of education with sufficient success to continue their studies in higher education institutions for anywhere between two and six years and then topped off their educational career in many cases with a period of internship, apprenticeship or probation before being admitted to membership of the profession through licensing by the state and/or acceptance into a learned society or professional organisation.

The professionals' educational career has focused on three major educational areas: the acquisition of knowledge, the development of skills, and the internalising of a set of values associated with membership of a profession. The educational process has allowed men and women to call themselves members of a particular profession. Therefore, education for them has been a means to an end rather than an end in itself. In other words, education has been instrumental. In summary, the educational process through which professionals have successfully progressed has been multi-dimensional and instrumental.

It can be argued, and is perhaps assumed, that continuing professional education — the process that continues past initial training and certification — is just a continuation of the initial educational process, that is, CPE is *more of the same*. However, there are complications that arise from this assumption. These complications can be considered under two headings: the professional and the professional association.

One set of complications focus on the individual professional. Initial training is essentially preparatory. Once the professional is a practitioner, there may be a feeling that he or she is 'trained' and thus the ethos of educational activity changes dramatically. What becomes of prime importance to the individual professional is his or her own practice as it operates day to day, in a particular work setting, in collaboration (or conflict) with professionals from the same or other professions and non-professionals, technical people or managers. Economic factors such as salary and income may assume a high profile. The professional may be working as a lone practitioner in a rural community or new housing development with little collegial contact. There may, in fact, be a questioning of some, or a great deal, of the content of initial training. While there may be nostalgic feelings about the camaraderie of initial training, post-initial training, that is, CPE needs to deal with professionals in a different setting.

If the professional association is to have a major role in the development of CPE, in contrast with a minor role in initial training, then the concerns of the association will play a role in CPE. If there are pressures to discipline the wayward practitioner; to improve the community image of the profession; to seek to protect boundaries; to reduce the impact of government imposts, then these pressures — when developed into association policies — are likely to impact on CPE. While the multi-dimensional and instrumental features of education that are evident in initial training may continue into CPE, it is suggested that the changed role of the student, now a professional, and the contribution of a professional association, rather than a higher education institution or institutions, with the association's wide responsibility for the sorts of factors proposed in Houle's process of professionalisation, then CPE will *not* be just a continuation of initial training.

In discussing two areas of potential complications when assuming that CPE can be just a continuation of initial training, the potential for conflict in CPE program objectives was also highlighted. There is a potential for conflict between the perception of CPE as primarily being concerned with assisting the individual practitioner to improve his or her performance or gain new skills, and being concerned with wider issues that relate to the autonomy, status and functioning of a profession in relation to other professions. It is suggested that this is one important dimension that needs to be considered in discussions of CPE.

It is also suggested that there will be continuities and discontinuities between initial training and CPE. Schein noted (Characteristic 2) that professionals are motivated. However, the level and type of motivation of the individual professional is likely to change from initial training to CPE. The three dimensions of initial professional preparation — knowledge, skills and professional values — are likely to continue but the approach to his or her education may be different. While new knowledge or skills may be seen as important, there may be requirements for new methodologies to be used in the teaching/learning process. While the professional values of the profession may remain important, these may be being challenged as the professional makes contact with other professionals and clients and is faced with the economic realities of practice. It is likely that the instrumental purpose of education will remain. Inservice education is likely to be seen as a means of becoming an even more competent practitioner. However, the former student, now a professional, is likely to place a high priority on the content and methodology he or she prefers and may give a low priority to those areas of CPE that are perceived as being priorities of the professional association or higher education institutions or his or her initial training.

The relationship between pre- and inservice professional education is important. The relationship may not always be clear, in the minds of the profession, the individual practitioner or those responsible for initial training. In terms of the discontinuities discussed above, the possibility should be available for the new practitioner's concern about limitations in his or her initial training to be mediated through CPE to result in modification to initial training programs.

The argument has been made that pre- and inservice professional education should not be considered separately. The concept of lifelong education is a major educational justification for the argument. Lifelong education supports the concept of education as not being concentrated on youth but being associated in different forms with different stages of the whole lifespan. The lifelong education concept provides a mechanism for examining the pre- and inservice education of professionals as an entity (see Dave, 1973; and Gelpi, 1985).

The Goals of CPE

Education is not politically neutral. Writers such as Freire (1972), Gelpi (1985), Thompson (1981) and Griffin (1983) have argued that the political nature of education is evident not just in the construction of knowledge and the choice of methodologies but more importantly in the degree to which the focus is on the individual (in contrast to the group or system or society as a whole) and the stance that is taken on the question of social change. In Freire's words: 'Does education domesticate or liberate?' (Freire, 1972, pp. 16–19).

While these theoretical formulations have related more to those in underdeveloped nations or to the so-called disadvantaged in developed nations, the issues are very pertinent to professionals and professional associations. There is the potential conflict between the demands of the individual practitioner and the requirement to accommodate wider social changes or seek to redress them. Gelpi (1985, p. 178), in discussing lifelong education, has identified two polarised positions for the real goals of education:

> On the one hand, there is education for development, creativity, invention, co-operation, democracy, participation, self-development, the search for significant values, freedom of expression for individuals and groups, the right of everyone to aesthetic experience, the satisfaction of needs both essential and 'non-essential'. On the other, education is an instrument of oppression, control, segregation, intolerance, to a greater or lesser extent covert racism, boredom, bureaucratisation, social reproduction, the triumph of platitudes, moralism, the reification of significant values. It is within this dialectic that, during the 1970s, the struggle developed concerning the research, theory, policy and practice of lifelong education.

What are the various stances that CPE can adopt in relation to these conflicting demands? Scanlan (Cervero & Scanlan, 1985, p. 15) proposes nine possible orientations for CPE in coping with the various demands (see Figure 2.2). One dimension of the orientations reflects the target levels of CPE: the individual professional practitioner, the professional organisation and the wider system, including other professions and occupational groups. The other dimension suggests three possible approaches: remediating deficiencies, fostering growth and facilitating change. The Scanlan approach avoids the strong distinction between domestication and liberation. The nine orientations allow for more precise assessment of the objectives of CPE, whether the objectives are explicit or implied.

Which of the nine orientations are evident in either CPE policy documents or statements or the CPE program as delivered? To what extent are association objectives, other than specifically labelled CPE, based on the goal orientations of Figure 2.2? Is the primary focus on the individual practitioner — the practitioner whose low level of competence puts him or her and the image of the profession at risk — with the prime objective of raising his or her level of performance? Or is the objective to make the whole profession more responsive to societal changes and expectations? While CPE may be expected to serve narrowly defined

	Remediating Deficiencies	Fostering Growth	Facilitating Change
Individual	Orientation 1 Updating/ competency assurance	Orientation 2 Individual growth	Orientation 3 Professional reorientation
Organisation	Orientation 4 Employee training	Orientation 5 Employee education	Orientation 6 Organisational development
System	Orientation 7 Systems deficit	Orientation 8 Systems improvement	Orientation 9 Systems reform

Figure 2.2 Goal Orientations of Continuing Professional Education
Source: *Problems and Prospects in Continuing Education* (R. M. Cervero and C. L. Scanlon (eds), 1985), p. 15.

goals related primarily to the technical competence of individual members, the nine orientations offer a wide scope for CPE in relation to overall association or profession-wide objectives.

Summary

CPE is a term relating to the post-initial training and induction of professionals. There are similarities and differences between preservice training and CPE. The concept of lifelong education, however, provides a basis for examining the professionals' education in a longitudinal manner. Because education's roles and goals have been conceptualised as having an active, rather than a neutral, relationship to social change, CPE has the possibility of playing a significant part in facilitating change in the wider social system as well as the profession itself and the individual members. Such a possibility should not be overlooked when professional practice in Australia is operating in a context of rapid change.

The question has been asked: 'Is CPE a *panacea, placebo or poison* for the professions in Australia?' (Brennan, 1987). Understanding the dynamics of social change and having far-reaching goals for CPE is of little value unless there are effective management and delivery systems to change such goals. In Chapter 3 we examine these important features of CPE.

References

Association of Professors of Higher Education. (1975). *Newsletter.* Washington: American Association for Higher Education.
Australian Bureau of Statistics & Department of Employment and Industrial Relations. (1987). *Australian standard classification of occupations dictionary.* Canberra: Australian Government Publishing Service.
Brennan, B. (1987). Continuing professional education: Panacea, placebo or poison for the professions. Paper presented at the 56th ANZAAS Conference, Palmerston North.
Cervero, R. M. & Scanlan, C L. (eds). (1985). *Problems and prospects in continuing professional education.* San Francisco: Jossey-Bass.
Daniel, A. (1983). *Power, privilege and prestige: Occupations in Australia.* Melbourne: Longman Cheshire.
Dave, R. H. (1973). *Lifelong education and the school curriculum.* Hamburg: UNESCO Institute for Education.
Dawkins, J. S. (1987). *Higher education: A policy discussion paper.* ('Dawkins' Green Paper'). Canberra: Australian Government Publishing Service.
Dawkins, J. S. (1988). *Higher education: A policy statement.* ('Dawkins White Paper'). Canberra: Australian Government Publishing Service.
Freire, P. (1972). *Pedagogy of the oppressed.* Harmondsworth: Penguin.
Gelpi, E. (1985). *Lifelong education and international relations.* London: Croom Helm.
Griffin, C. (1983). *Curriculum theory in adult and lifelong education.* London: Croom Helm.
Houle, C. O. (1980). *Continuing learning in the professions.* San Francisco: Jossey-Bass.
Illich, I. et al. (1977). *The disabling professions.* London: Marion Boyars.
Jarvis, P. (1983). *Professional education.* London: Croom Helm.
Partlett, D. F. (1985). *Professional negligence.* North Ryde, NSW: Law Book Company.
Schein, E. H. (1972). *Professional education.* New York: McGraw-Hill.
Thompson, J. L. (ed.). *Education for a change.* London: Hutchinson.
Woll, B. (1984). The empty ideal: A critique of 'continuing learning in the professions'. In the *Adult Education Quarterly,* **34**,(3) 167–177.

3
A Framework for Discussing CPE

BARRIE BRENNAN

This chapter provides a framework for the professional profiles that follow in Chapters 4 to 8 inclusive. In the context of Australia in the closing decades of the 20th century, what does CPE mean and how does it operate? What are successes and what have been the problems? What future directions are indicated?

The discussion of this chapter and the ones that follow is based on six sets of considerations related to CPE: contextual factors, policy and objectives (including the voluntary or mandatory (compulsory) issue), management, program content and delivery, evaluation and finance (Brennan, 1988). General background information is provided from the results of a survey conducted in connection with what is believed to have been the first major national conference on CPE in Australia, held in 1987. All professions and professional organisations contacted were asked to complete a simple 12-item survey. Fifty responses were received, 47 of which were usable. Additional responses have been received since the conference. While an analysis of the responses has been produced in the conference proceedings (Dymock, 1988), select data, some more up-to-date than those in the proceedings, is set out in Table 3.1 on the following page. The data from the survey does not purport to be representative. The professional population covered was 122,000, compared with the labour force total of 867,000. At the moment, however, this survey is the most reliable source of comparative data available for the Australian scene — hence its being frequently quoted in the following pages.

Table 3.1 Data from CPE Survey, 1988

1 Respondent associations

Health-related	24		
Law	4		
Accounting	3	National associations	31
Engineering	4	State-based associations	16
Education	4		
Ungrouped	8	These 47 associations represented
Total	47	122,000 professionals.

2 CPE personnel in management and delivery

Full-time staff	79	Qualifications
Part-time staff	37	>200 were qualified in host organisation's profession; 41 were qualified in CPE.
Volunteers	>350	

3 Content of CPE activities

New techniques/procedures	37
New theoretical knowledge	33
Management/supervisory skills	28
Ethical problems	26
Legal/administrative problems	19
Liberal studies	3
Other	11

4 Cooperation with other agencies in aspects of programming

	Tertiary institutions	Other professions	Government agencies	Private consultants	Consumers/ public
Policy		9	5	5	5
Management	11	7	6	6	3
Program delivery	24	22	13	18	7
Evaluation	13	8	6	9	13

5 Source of finance for CPE activities[a]

No. of sources[b]	One	Two	Three	Four
No. of organisations	14[c]	20	4	2

Notes: (a) Only 40 of the 47 organisations responding to the survey answered Item 5; (b) The five options for source of finance were participants, employers, the association, government, and industry; (c) Of these 14, 10 relied on participants, 3—the association, and 1—government.

Source: Responses to the 1987 survey, CPE Conference, Armidale, NSW. University of New England, Department of Continuing Education.

Contextual factors

In examining CPE in a specific profession there are four contextual factors that are relevant: history and special features; demography of the profession; initial training and licensing; and the role of the professional association.

Professions cannot disregard their history, however long or short it may be. There may be important elements in their history that point to issues in CPE. Has the profession established its identity by splitting off from another group? Has the profession, as the result of specialisation, witnessed the splintering off of new professions? Part of the socialisation process that is professionalisation should involve an understanding of origin — the profession's history.

Demographic data for the professions in Australia was given in Chapter 2. Those persons concerned with CPE should have a very detailed, up-to-date picture of the composition of their profession. As a minimum, data on age, sex, country of origin and income should be maintained. Also required is information on those not currently employed, where members practise, and the nature of their work. Information that can identify major sub-groups within the profession should also be noted.

The survey asked about numbers in the profession, and percentages involved in CPE offered by the profession and other organisations. The responses to these questions suggest that either the data is not recorded or that it is not easily retrieved. Only 18 responses answered these questions; many of them were estimates.

Changes within the higher education sector as a result of the ministerial White Paper (Dawkins, 1988) will result in alterations to the initial training programs for many professions. The consolidation of institutions, for example, will result in the disappearance of many institutions as separate entities. It is relevant, then, for those persons involved in CPE to have information about past and present programs of initial training for the profession, from the various institutions. Associated with initial training is the question of licensing or gaining the right to practise, and the increasingly important requirement of re-licensing. In the area of initial training and licensing, information needs to be held or be able to be accessed on these questions in all Australian states and in overseas countries because of population mobility within Australia and immigration respectively.

The fourth contextual factor that needs to be considered in relation to CPE is the question of the role of the professional association. Schein and the North American Higher Education Professors both recognised the important role of the professional association in relation to professional life. What is the role, then, of the professional association in general, and more specifically in CPE? If, as seems to be the case for Australian teachers, there is no group that is the equivalent of the professional organisation, what agency or agencies fill the void in general professional matters and in CPE?

Where the professional organisation has a written history, this may provide some clues as to its ability to adjust to changing roles and its general reaction to wider social and economic changes. What is the role of the professional association in licensing, discipline, initial training, re-licensing, relations with other professions, and as a lobby group? Has the professional association, overtly or obliquely, adopted a professionalising mission such as that advocated by Houle (1980)?

If the profession has an increasing proportion of employees, is the professional association moving more in the direction of a trade union? What are the general implications for the association and for CPE from such a trend?

Policy and objectives

It is assumed that the professional association will have a major responsibility for CPE, with teachers a notable exception. The history of CPE in a profession, whether long or short, may illustrate important policy shifts and reflect factors that have influenced changes. For example, have the changes from an interpersonal to a legal relationship between professional and client or recognised changes in the composition of the profession or technological changes in professional practice been influential factors in shifts of policy?

For an interpretation of CPE in a profession, the existence of a policy document or statement or series of principles is important. The process, including the personnel involved, in the development of a policy document illustrates by implication the importance of CPE in the profession and gives an indication as to whether CPE is a central or peripheral concern, or whether it is associated with a movement to control the profession.

In the 1988 survey 26 respondents (that is, 52 per cent of all respondents) indicated that there was a policy document. Many responding professional organisations included a copy of their 'document', which in size and scope ranged from a single sheet, setting out either general principles or types of approved CPE activities, to comprehensive material such as a series of printed booklets describing the rationale, purpose and methods of CPE as defined by the profession. The vast range of documents illustrates not only the different stages that the various professions have reached in CPE policy development but also the level of sophistication developed to justify, manage and evaluate CPE. As important as the initial drawing up of a policy document for CPE are the methods envisaged for its review and modification. In the assessment of the policy documents, attention can also be given to apparent influences on the document. Has an overseas model or the practice of another profession been adopted? Has a significant individual, strategic committee, state group, higher education institution or sub-group within the profession had marked influence on the document? In the documents submitted as part of the survey, there was evidence for most of these influences. However, the major trend was for professions to have opted for a similar document to that produced by their own profession overseas, most usually from North America.

The *objectives* of a profession's CPE can be considered in many ways and at various levels. Do the objectives have some congruence with the broad range of objectives described by Houle as the professionalisation process? As an option to checking objectives against the Houle list, another approach, described in Chapter 2, can be used. Because of the direction of the profession's CPE objectives, which of the Scanlan orientations (see Figure 2.2 in Chapter 2) appear to be most in evidence? Where is the emphasis in relation to the individual practitioner: on remediation or developing competence? Are objectives related to the system? What attitude is evident with regard to change — fostering or facilitating? Is the target of CPE primarily the individual practitioner or wider social systems? Also, the objectives can be checked against those that were suggested as being the focus of initial training. To what extent is the emphasis on knowledge, skills or socialisation?

Because professions do not operate in a social vacuum, CPE objectives should be examined for the degree to which they seek to accommodate factors such as policy initiatives from government or changes in general social conditions and community behaviour. Do the objectives recognise an increase in litigation against the profession's members for negligence? Is there an emphasis on accommodating changes in government policy at both the federal and state levels?

National government 'interest' in the professions was noted in Chapter 2 in relation to the labour market. In a more direct link with CPE, there have been developments relating to training of professions. In 1986, the Commonwealth Tertiary Education Commission (CTEC) commissioned an enquiry into adult and continuing education (Johnson & Hinton, 1985, 1986). Continuing professional education was included by the writers as part of their brief. However, they noted that the field of adult and continuing education was so vast that special areas, such as CPE, required enquiries of their own. They recommended either a review of the whole field or discipline enquiries (Johnson & Hinton, 1986, p. 6). No indication has been given in either CTEC documents or in the ministerial White Paper (Dawkins, 1988) that an overall enquiry will be undertaken.

Policy development at the national level for CPE is likely to emerge piecemeal from discipline reviews (Johnson, 1988). Four discipline enquiries have been initiated at the national level focusing on the law, medicine, engineering, and teacher education in mathematics and science. The law review (Pearce, 1987) stressed the initial training for the profession in the law schools but continuing education was included in the terms of reference for the review and in the report. The report criticised some law schools for the quality of initial training for the profession and recommended the promotion of the role of continuing legal education, especially for new practitioners. The overall role of CPE, though noted as important, was viewed as less than that discussed in Chapter 2.

The enquiry into the medical workforce (Doherty, 1988), where the target group was defined narrowly to include only medical practitioners and omitted all other professions in the ASCO category of health diagnosis and treatment practitioners, had as part of its brief to make recommendations on continuing medical education. The recommendations emphasise two points: that, as a condition of continuing registration to practise, medical practitioners must belong to an accredited group with a major responsibility for continuing education, and that there was a need for the coordination of continuing medical education. These two recommendations can be interpreted as indicating a movement towards *mandatory* continuing education and the development of an overall program of CPE, two issues raised below.

Continuing professional education was also included in the terms of reference of the engineering review (Williams, 1988). In the review's report considerable attention was placed on the human and social aspects of technological change and on the need to address these aspects in initial training. The report does not devote much attention to CPE. In fact, only two pages (pp. 34-35) are devoted to CPE and the single recommendation refers only to greater employer support for CPE. There is a more lengthy discussion of CPE in the specialised sections of the report, for example under 'mechanical engineering' within the section on curriculum and teaching. In the report, there is no recommendation that CPE can, or should, make a major contribution to the solution of major problems in the profession as a whole in dealing with social, economic and environmental, as well as technological, problems associated with adjustment to change.

At the time of writing, the review of education for teachers of mathematics and science is gathering evidence and no report has been issued. In its terms of reference, mention is made of 'inservice awards', 'professional development' and 'post-experience award programs' (Speedy, 1988). The context for this review is the requirement for a supply of well-trained students from the school system for tertiary courses in engineering, science and technology in terms of national economic goals. What the review will recommend in terms of CPE for teachers in these fields is unknown.

What is significant to note, from the setting of the teachers' review and the context of the reports of the other reviews, is that discipline reviews are likely to place high priority on some of the issues raised in Chapter 2 (labour-market factors, the demographics of the professions, and initial training) and will be set within national social and economic goals. The evidence from the discipline reviews is that CPE is considered as only a marginal factor in professional practice and has a role more limited than was suggested in Chapter 2. There is scope, however, for professional associations who have a clear set of objectives for CPE, and can produce evidence of success in reaching these objectives through CPE, to seek to influence further discipline enquiries regarding a wider role for CPE.

The White Paper (Dawkins, 1988), which indicates a major change in higher education, but does not mention CPE as a specific area, and the various professional enquiries noted above, will need to be addressed by those persons who develop CPE policy and objectives. If an overall review of CPE is not envisaged, then generalisations for the whole field are likely to be made from single discipline evidence. However, the discipline reviews may not be able to encapsulate many of the important changes related to newer disciplines/professions or that are impinging on traditional professions in their contemporary practice. The White Paper's impact will certainly be noticeable in the initial training of professionals. Policy objectives for professional CPE need to recognise not only what initial training has been, and is, but also what initial training may become.

While much attention has been given to policy development at the national level, the role of state governments cannot be overlooked, because it is at the state level that most professions are registered or given leave to practise. General policies at the state level for CPE have not been developed. There is not always agreement from one state to another regarding the need for regulation or certification. Currently, the state of New South Wales is discussing the issue of registering psychologists. Other states have already established a system for registration. There is no requirement that New South Wales should follow the regulations set down in other states. As a result the many relevant questions about who is acceptable for registration (and therefore who is ineligible), what training is required and from what institution, what level of accountability is required for advice or treatment, may receive different answers in different states? Even the issue of continuing professional education has to be settled. In this process the professional association, the Australian Psychologists' Association, seeks to play a prominent role.

The states have only recently moved to the stage of developing policy statements on the broader field of adult and continuing education — for example in New South Wales (Cavalier, 1986). It is therefore unlikely that the states will take the initiative to develop a specific policy to cover the range of professions with respect to CPE, particularly as there is little coordination in the long-established area of professional certification.

Voluntary or Mandatory (compulsory) CPE?

For many writers on CPE and many professionals involved in CPE or ordinary practice, the major, for some the only, policy issue in CPE is

A FRAMEWORK FOR DISCUSSING CPE 41

Table 3.2 Trends in Mandatory CPE in the USA for Twelve Professions, 1977–88

Profession	1987	1980	1984	1986	1988
Architect	0	1/1	1/6	1/6	1/6
CPA	23	36/1	43/1	47	48
Dentist	8	9/1/1	10/0/1	13	14
Engineer	0	1/1	1/1	1/1	1/1
Lawyer	7	9/8	12/0/8	20/0/4	31
Optometrist	45	44	46	46	48
Psychologist		8/6	12/9	13/8	16/8
Pharmacist	14	21	30/3	38/3	39
Physical therapist		3	3/1	7/1/1	8
Physician	17/11	20/4/1	18/4/1	21/4/1	22
Social worker	6	10	18	20/7/1	23/4/2
Veterinarian	18	22	24/1	26/2	26/2

Note: The first digit represents the number of states with mandatory requirements; the second digit, the number of states with enabling legislation passed; and the third digit, the number of states with requirements under certain circumstances.

Source: Personal communication from Dr Louis E. Phillips, 15 July 1988.

whether CPE should be voluntary or mandatory. The voluntary versus mandatory debate has been waged in the general literature covering a number of professions, and in specific professions. (The legal profession in New South Wales has been included in the series of professional profiles that follow partly because it has embraced compulsory CPE.) The debate has been acrimonious. Data has been assembled from time to time to support both sides of the debate. So as to provide an uncommitted point of view in this chapter, date is reproduced on developments relating to mandatory CPE in the USA in the early 1980s, in Table 3.2 (Phillips, L. E., 1988, pers. comm. 15 July). Both sides can draw their own conclusions from the data.

In summary, the arguments are as follows. If a voluntary system is adopted, then the practitioners most likely to need CPE are the least likely to become involved. So if CPE is mandatory everyone is involved and the profession can indicate this to governments, licensing authorities and the public. The whole level of the profession can be raised. Opponents of mandatory CPE argue that people *cannot be forced* to learn; the unwilling participant will attend but not learn. Others will learn to play the system. Rather than simply giving additional power over the profession to those members who control CPE, the challenge is to have programs of such quality and relevance that members will want to attend and participate (see Dymock, 1988; Maple, 1987).

Whether or not a profession has committed itself to the mandatory or voluntary approach, here is a point of policy that needs to be resolved and which is related to many of the points raised in the debate. Do the policy objectives cite particular priority groups for CPE? Are these groups the incompetent or the lone, distant practitioners or those in government employ or those in cross-disciplinary teams or those with non-Australian backgrounds or women who have had a period out of the workforce? While a variety of priority groups may be identified, the rationale and objectives must be sought for the identification of these groups. Are they sought because the profession views its responsibility as a service role with those groups or is there an implied assumption that such groups may contain potentially incompetent practitioners? Are the members of the identified groups those who should be first in line for mandatory CPE, the at-risk practitioners who will be the potential cases for negligence? Control motivations are central to many issues in CPE.

While the mandatory versus voluntary issue may be the major concern to professions in the development of their CPE policy, there are at least three other questions of equal importance: How broadly, or narrowly, is education defined in policy? What is the position, explicit or implicit, taken in the policy objectives in relation to the nine orientations delineated by Scanlan (see Figure 2.2, Chapter 2)? Is there evidence from the policy and objectives that control of the membership is a goal for CPE? Concentration on the policy issue of mandatory versus voluntary tends to cloud other policy issues, of equal or greater significance.

Management

The finest policy document is of little use without an adequate and appropriate management system. There is a problem for many Australian professional associations because of differences in state policies, for example regarding registration of professions. Because of the importance of state differences for some professions, there is the management structure of general policy and decision-making at the national level and the policy interpretation and implementation at state level.

The federal level of management cannot be overlooked. The interest of the Federal Government in areas such as the labour market and higher education requires an interest by professional organisations in national policies.

At either the national or state level, the status of CPE can be viewed as a measure of the management structure adopted. If CPE has a central status with eminent persons as ex-officio members of the committee, then its status appears to be high. If however, it has a structure and membership parallel in importance to such activities as those with the responsibility of deciding the next venue for the annual conference or who shall be on the judging panel for this prize or that award, then perhaps its status can be questioned.

Other measures of the centrality of CPE can be judged by the amount of time devoted to the subject by the national executive or at the annual conference, or the amount of editorial space that is devoted to the subject in the professional association's journal and other publications.

The normal pattern is for CPE to be managed at the national and state levels by a sub-committee of the national or state executive. The membership of the sub-committee, usually association members, may be as a result of an election or composed of volunteers. There is some evidence that outsiders are being invited to join such committees, for example, representatives of higher education institutions, people from other professions, members of specific sub-groups within the professions or even the general public. The legal profession in New South Wales has placed advertisements in the press calling for lay participants in various committees of its governing body.

Those concerned with CPE in a profession can make their own judgements of the importance of CPE by examining the membership of the CPE sub-committee. Who are the members? What is their status and experience? What sections, if any, of the profession do they represent? Is there evidence, or even a suspicion, that control of the profession may be being sought through the CPE 'back door'?

Management structures for CPE in professional organisations in Australia tend to reflect the overall management structure of the organisation. The special needs of CPE are generally not reflected in the management structure.

In the area of CPE program delivery, the general developmental pattern has been for a member to be appointed part-time to organise the activities of the CPE program. As the work develops, the position may become full-time, usually with the same person staying on to take on the full-time position. At a later stage when other personnel are required, people from outside the profession, with appropriate educational qualifications (or specifically adult education qualifications) may be employed in addition to or in place of members of the profession.

The 1988 survey indicated that the majority of professional organisations used persons with expertise in their own professional area. The survey also indicated that extensive use was made of part-timers for CPE, either from the profession or as employees. Seventy-nine full-time and 37 part-time staff were engaged in CPE in the professions responding. The vast majority of the 116 staff had qualifications in the host profession's expertise, and 41 had some training in CPE specifically.

Program content and delivery

There are many offerings under the CPE banner in Australia. Reading the journals and newsletters of the professional associations, the columns of the educational magazines or even the daily press provides many examples of courses, workshops, seminars, etc. Two general, related questions arise from all these offerings: Is there an overall design in all the offerings?; and How do these offerings relate to the objectives of the CPE program?

In the discussion of content and delivery, a distinction is made between the many individual offerings or 'activities', and the total offerings or 'program'. Rephrased the questions are: How do all the activities contribute to the program?; and How does the program match with the objectives of CPE for a particular profession? What evidence is there of Houle's professionalisation or Scanlan's orientations?

One means of gaining answers to the questions posed above is to ask a further question: How are activities selected? An illustration to answer this last question gives answers also to the earlier questions. A committee at a regional level (diocese, synod, or presbytery are not mentioned so as to protect the identity of the organisation) is discussing, as is their brief, CPE for the regional clergy for the forthcoming year. The question is asked about the visitors to the region. The answer given results in a discussion of what these important visitors can be asked to talk about for the local clergy. The list of visitors has added to it a series of activities in which they are resource people and the CPE program for the year is finally drawn up. Such a procedure is hardly likely, in a planned way, to satisfy any anticipated CPE objectives, other than providing activities that keep the visitors and regional clergy busy.

In seeking to provide a better procedure and make some impact on CPE program objectives, professions have used the concept of *needs analysis*. What are the needs of the practitioners out there? How can they be met? How can they be balanced with the needs of the organisation and the profession as a whole?

Past experience is often the key determinant of CPE program content. Activities that have been successful in the past tend to be repeated, with regard to either content or method. If a clinical workshop day has produced an enrolment of 200 and a similar activity on the development of practice-based research attracts only ten persons, then the responses to the two activities are likely to influence later offerings.

The survey of professional associations sought information on the content of the CPE programs (Table 3.1, Item 3). New techniques/procedures with 37 responses and new theoretical knowledge with 33 responses were the most common content areas reported of the six listed in the survey. The variety of content in the CPE programs surveyed is illustrated by responses to the 'other' category: professional issues, old knowledge, communication skills, quality assurance, assessment and evaluation, behaviour modification, group work, lobbying, comparative studies, personal development. There is apparently a wide variety of offerings in the content of CPE programs across the professions.

Methodology cannot be overlooked in the delivery of a program. It was argued above that CPE was not just a continuation of initial training. Perhaps, there is also a requirement for changes in methodology from initial training where the norm has been lectures and demonstrations together with clinical supervision or supervised practice. Has there been a conscious effort to foster involvement by the professional practitioner in the CPE activities? Have some of the practices of adult education been adopted as policy? Has a link between the type of content being discussed and methodology been examined?

If one of the reasons for the increased attention to CPE has been the development of new technology, has the new technology of teaching and learning been incorporated, where relevant, into the CPE delivery system? The development of distance education that has come with technological advances, and the improved techniques for delivering information through computer-assisted learning should not be overlooked.

One of the developments in North America, supported by the Kellogg Foundation, involves the *collaboration of agencies* in the delivery of CPE programs. Is there evidence of cooperative and collaborative arrangements for the delivery of CPE programs or is CPE a field of unnecessary duplication? In the delivery of programs, is there collaboration with other professions, government departments, higher education institutions, or private consultancies? Are packages in areas that are common to many professions, for example, in interpersonal skills, being used, or is every profession doing its own thing, with many possibilities that the education wheel is being re-invented again and again in separate professions?

The 1988 survey indicated that, in the delivery of CPE programs in Australia, there is a good deal of collaborative and cooperative effort — see Table 3.1, Item 4. The degree of cooperation that was indicated in the survey is at its highest level in relation to program delivery (again see Table 3.1). A problem, then, for the professional association may be in relation to the degree of control and coordination it can maintain over the activities delivered by this variety of agencies. Does the professional association have, or need to develop, a process for recognising or accrediting either providers or programs? Or do professional associations leave decisions about the suitability or value of programs to their individual members or their employers, or perhaps to the operations of the market place?

In the delivery of CPE programs, the front-line troops are the lecturers, tutors and facilitators. Because of their vital role, some attention needs to be given to a monitoring process for their evaluation. In overviewing the CPE program, a useful exercise is to examine the *sources* of CPE instructional personnel. Are they predominantly from higher education institutions or drawn from key members of the profession? Is extensive use made of overseas experts? Is a cadre of CPE-providers being developed? What sort of guidance and assistance is given to the instructors and leaders? Is too little assistance given? Is too much expected of them? Do the program planners leave too much responsibility to the chief presenters of the activities?

While the apparent increase in CPE activities may be considered 'a good sign', the amount of activity needs to be judged in terms of the degree to which it is designed to meet specific objectives, the degree to which it is meeting individual and professional needs and the degree to which it is not encouraging duplication of activities and the waste of resources.

Evaluation

The question of judging the CPE program was raised in the previous section. Evaluation is concerned with making judgements about the value of individual CPE activities and of CPE programs as a whole. It is not a question of whether or not those involved in the management or delivery of CPE programs are centrally concerned about the evaluation of the CPE program or not, because others will make their judgements about the value and effectiveness of the program. The individual practitioners are likely to test out the CPE offerings of their profession. If they do not meet their needs then it it likely that they will be less willing to register for future activities. But professionals do not live in a vacuum, and the consumers of professional services and governments and other professions also will make evaluative judgements of the effectiveness of a profession's CPE program.

Does the CPE program offer any guarantees? What do terms such as 'quality control' (Groteleuschen, 1986) mean in operational terms and in relation to evaluation? Can anyone define *a competent practitioner*?

While the CPE program developer can have only minimal impact on the judgements that are made by those outside the profession, what is vital is that the objectives of the profession's CPE program are expressed in clear terms so that they can be a basis for evaluation. The objectives of the total program can then be evaluated in the context of the specific activities of the program and in terms of the way these objectives are expressed in terms of the individual needs of the particular profession's membership.

Whether or not the profession has adopted a mandatory policy, one of the requirements is that the CPE program deliverers need to have comprehensive records of activities, of those who attend, of their learning and of the degree of success (or failure) of the activity. In addition, if professions were to encourage their members to participate in activities from other agencies, then these too would have to be monitored and recorded.

Finance

Good education programs are not cheap. The conduct of an effective CPE program, well staffed, thoroughly planned and effectively promoted, efficiently presented and evaluated, and conducted in good educational surroundings, or delivered via audio or video tape or teleconference, is an expensive business. How is such a program to be financed?

Since professionals are in the higher economic brackets and CPE contributes to their earning power as practitioners, then they should perhaps be expected to pay for their CPE. The 1988 survey indicated that while other sources — employers, the association, government and industry subsidies — contributed to financing the CPE program, most activities relied on the payment of fees by participants.

The evidence from the survey (Table 3.1 Item 5), is that, of the 40 organisations who responded to the item, 65 per cent use two or more sources to finance their CPE programs. Of the 14 professions using only one method, 71 per cent rely on the participant to pay for the activities' costs.

If it could be assumed that professionals work in private practice, then the previous expectation — that they should finance their own CPE — may be acceptable. However, as the labour force figures indicated, most Australian professionals in the ASCO classification of professional are employees. The question arises, then, as to whether or not employers should contribute to the CPE costs of their employees because their corporation or department is also likely to benefit from the enhanced knowledge and skills of the practitioner. The impression gained by CPE providers is that cheques for CPE activities tend to come from employers rather than individuals. This impression conflicts with the results of the survey but does reflect the fact that the vast majority of professionals in Australia are employees.

If CPE is to develop the labour force, and the ASCO definition of professional emphasised *on-the-job training*, then is there not a case for government financial support for at least some CPE programs that are associated with government priority areas? There is both government and community support for CPE through tax deductibility for personal educational activities. However, those persons able to benefit most from the deductions are the ones in the higher taxation brackets.

The *user-pays* principle may inhibit the participation of some practitioners in some professions. Add-on costs to the actual cost of the program — travel, accommodation, arrangements for child care, etc — may act as a barrier to participation. Practitioners living in remote areas or with family responsibilities may be prevented from participating by cost factors. Such barriers may be the reason for the non-participation of special target groups for a profession's CPE. Some analysis of participation may indicate the presence of cost barriers.

There are sources other than government from which funds may be gained to support or sponsor CPE. The professions have contacts with the private sector — the companies that supply the equipment, drugs, books, resource material, and technical apparatus. Some associations have successfully explored the sponsorship of various CPE activities by commercial enterprises such as the visit of an overseas expert, demonstrations of new equipment. While caution has to be exercised that sponsorship or the use of equipment does not necessarily mean blanket approval for the company or its equipment (that is, ethical compromise), private commercial sponsorship may provide associations with flexibility in the financing of activities. Gaining sponsorship for CPE activities may allow for flexibility in financing activities in general or for the subsidising of special activities or the provision of scholarships for practitioners in targetted need groups.

In CPE, effective financial management is a vital factor in the overall management and delivery. The variability and status of the CPE operation within the association may be determined as much by the financial as the educational management of CPE.

References

Brennan, B. (1988). Challenges to continuing professional education in Australia. In D. Dymock (ed.), *Continuing professional education — Policy and provision.* Armidale: University of New England, Department of Continuing Education.

Cavalier, R. (1986). *The provision of adult education in New South Wales.* Sydney: Ministry of Education.

Dawkins, J. S. (1988). *Higher education: A policy statement.* ('Dawkins' White Paper'). Canberra: Australian Government Publishing Service.

Doherty, R. (1988). *Australian medical education and workforce in the twenty-first century.* Canberra: Department of Community Services and Health, & Australian Government Publishing Service.

Dymock, D. (1988). *Continuing professional education — Policy and Provision.* Proceedings of the 1987 Conference on CPE in Australia, Armidale. Armidale: University of New England, Department of Continuing Education.

Groteleuschen, A. D. (1986). *Quality assurance in continuing professional education.* Occasional Papers, No. 2. Athens, G.A.: University of Georgia, Department of Adult Education.

Houle, C. O. (1980). *Continuing learning in the professions.* San Francisco: Jossey-Bass.

Johnson, R. (1988). Emerging government policy on continuing professional education and the place of discipline reviews. Paper presented at National CPE Conference, Armidale, September.

Johnson, R., & Hinton F. (1985). *Adult and continuing education in Australia.* Canberra: Commonwealth Tertiary Education Commission.

Johnson, R., & Hinton, F. (1986). *It's human nature: Non-award adult and continuing education in Australia.* Canberra: Commonwealth Tertiary Education Commission.

Maple, G. (1987). Continuing education for the health sciences: The voluntary/mandatory debate. *Australian Journal of Education,* 27(2), 22–28.

Pearce, D. (convenor). (1987). *Australian law schools.* Canberra: Australian Government Publishing Service.

Scanlan, C. L. (1985). Practising with purpose: Goals of continuing professional education. In R. M. Cervero, & C. L. Scanlan, (eds), *Problems and prospects in continuing professional education.* San Francisco: Jossey-Bass.

Speedy, G. W. (chairman). (1988). Letter containing Terms of Reference for the Discipline Review of Teacher Education in Mathematics and Science, 2 August.

Williams, B. (chairman). (1988). *Review of the discipline of engineering,* 3 vols. Canberra: Australian Government Publishing Service.

Part Two
CPE IN PRACTICE: THE PROFESSIONAL PROFILES

4
The Legal Profession

JOHN W. NELSON

Contextual factors

It is impractical within the ambit of this profile to provide a detailed coverage of the CPE provision for lawyers throughout the whole of Australia. The federal system of government in Australia has resulted in separate legal systems in each state and territory with most lawyers being admitted to practise in only one of them. This has led to eight independently structured and regulated legal professions, each with its own professional association. Although the CPE issues are essentially the same for all, these bodies have addressed them in varying ways, giving rise to a considerable diversity in provision. For these reasons this profile concentrates on the position in just one state, New South Wales. Not only does it possess the largest profession, but it is also distinguished by being the only state to have embarked upon mandatory CPE for solicitors, as well as a scheme of voluntary continuing judicial education.

One further problem in describing the field is that the legal profession consists of three branches: judges, barristers and solicitors, the last two being fused in some jurisdictions. Because the overwhelming majority of lawyers in New South Wales are solicitors and their CPE provision is the most highly developed, the focus in this chapter is on the operation of their mandatory Continuing Legal Education (CLE) scheme.

In contrast, there is very little CLE provision specifically for barristers. The Bar Association conducts only a handful of activities each year and advises that there is little demand for more. Perhaps this is because the high levels of expertise within the profession tend to reside in the bar. However, barristers are frequently presenters of CPE for solicitors and one can safely assume that some of them voluntarily attend many of the solicitors' CLE offerings.

One very interesting development in the field of CLE in New South Wales relates to continuing judicial education. One of the functions of the recently established Judicial Commission is to 'organise and supervise an appropriate scheme for the continuing education and training of judicial officers', which term embraces judges and magistrates. Participation is voluntary. The Commission has appointed an education director, who has conducted a survey of the learning needs of all judicial officers in the state with a view to developing appropriate activities for them (Riches, 1988). New South Wales is the first Australian state to take this step, but there is ample American precedent for it. Although for judges and magistrates the scheme is still very much in its infancy, it has generated much interest throughout the legal profession.

Law has possessed none of the problems with professional identity experienced by professions which have arrived more recently on the scene: it is acknowledged as one of the three traditional 'learned' professions (Schein, 1972). Its history in New South Wales is a long one, dating back to the early days of the colony. However, it did not fully emerge until after 1824 when the Supreme Court of New South Wales was established with the power to admit barristers and solicitors to practise in the colony (Bennett, 1984). The Law Society of New South Wales, the current title of the solicitors' professional association, can be traced back to 1884.

An appreciation of the composition of the profession can be gained through an analysis of solicitor numbers. Currently there are 10,000 practising solicitors in New South Wales. The conventional image of the typical solicitor as a relatively autonomous self-employed practitioner in a small suburban law firm can safely be relegated to the past. Only 16 per cent are in sole practice and a further 33 per cent in partnership. On the other hand, almost an equal number are employees in solicitors' offices (27 per cent) or in government service (10 per cent) or in legal positions with corporate employers (7 per cent). There is a growing trend towards larger law firms and more intense specialisation. As regards location, 48 per cent are practising in the city of Sydney, 26 per cent in the suburbs and 17 per cent in the country. Whereas the present position is that only 18 per cent are women, for those entering the profession the proportions of the sexes are now approaching parity. These sorts of data contain important clues for CPE providers. As Brennan (1988) has stressed, if the profession is going to be served by CPE, reliable and up-to-date information on its membership is essential.

The functions of the Law Society fall under two headings which, some would say, are potentially in conflict. First, it acts as a representative of its members in promoting their interests in relation to third parties. Second, it has a regulatory function which enables it to exercise a high level of control over solicitors. It is responsible for licensing them. All solicitors engaging in practice are obliged by law to hold a practising certificate issued by the Law Society of which they are thereby entitled to membership. The Society has the power to cancel practising certificates and to initiate disciplinary proceedings for professional misconduct, leading in some cases to the penalty of striking the delinquent off the roll of solicitors. One of the Society's principal concerns is the preservation and enhancement of its members' competence to practise and it has placed a great deal of faith in CPE to achieve this purpose.

Policy and objectives of CLE

The provision of CLE has burgeoned only during the past 15 years. Until the late 1960s, apart from occasional seminars offered by the Law Society and the University of Sydney, there was almost no formal CLE available in New South Wales. The individual lawyer addressed the problem of keeping up-to-date with changes in the law through his or her own self-directed study. The establishment of the College of Law by the Law Society in 1973 represented the first major commitment by the profession to CLE (Mackay, 1981). While the primary responsibility of the College was to provide a pre-admission course of practical legal training for law graduates, it had the secondary objective of developing a program of CLE for solicitors. Since that time there has been a growing recognition within the ranks of the profession of the need for continuing learning throughout the practising life of the solicitor. The important role to be assigned to CLE in assisting practitioners to address the challenges posed by the escalating pace of change in the nature of legal practice has also come to be widely acknowledged.

Voluntary or Mandatory?

Until 1987 participation in formal CLE was voluntary. During this period there was a large variety of quality CLE activities on offer which would have met the educational needs of most practising solicitors. However, the Law Society became concerned that those with the most acute need for improving their level of performance seldom attended these activities. It decided in 1986 to introduce a scheme of Mandatory CLE, following the resolution of the Council of the Law Society to adopt in substance the recommendations contained in the Fox Report (Law Society of New South Wales, 1985). This report had been commissioned by the Society to provide background material for Mandatory CLE and to suggest a scheme for its implementation. Undoubtedly the existence, when the proposal was under consideration in 1985, of Mandatory CLE in some sixteen states in the United States (Edwards, 1985), where in some cases it had been in operation for more than ten years, had been very persuasive in the decision to adopt a similar scheme in New South Wales.

The element of compulsion was effected by statute through an amendment to the Legal Practitioners Act (subsequently carried over into the Legal Profession Act, 1987). The power is conferred upon the Law Society to refuse to isssue or to cancel a solicitor's practising certificate (without which he or she cannot practise law) if that solicitor fails in the opinion of the Council of the Society to satisfy the requirement to undertake a minimum level of participation in certain approved educational activities. A Mandatory Continuing Legal Education Board was constituted to administer the scheme on behalf of the Society.

As a precondition for maintaining practising certificates, all solicitors are obliged to complete each twelve month period from 1 April to 31 March ten CLE units, as accredited by the Board. These units can comprise a variety of activities:

- One CLE unit may be obtained for each period of 60 minutes of participation in a program taking the form of lectures, discussions, demonstrations or 'similar activities'.
- One-half CLE unit may be secured for each period of 60 minutes of private or group instruction by accredited video cassette, video tape or audio tape, provided that no more than five units may be obtained in this manner.

- One CLE unit is available for each period of 60 minutes of video tape presentation conducted in conjunction with a speaker and/or commentator.
- CLE units can be obtained by writing an article of more than 2,000 words published in a legal or other approved journal or writing or presenting a paper to an accredited program.

However, the scheme gives no formal credit for any other learning styles, such as self-directed study not involving accredited video or audio tapes, for example, reading.

As evidence of compliance, solicitors are required at the time of their annual application for renewal of their practising certificates to indicate by statutory declaration whether they have completed their Mandatory CLE requirements during the previous twelve months. No other verification is demanded at this stage. However, the Board has foreshadowed (Mandatory CLE Board, 1987) that practitioners will from time to time be randomly called on to furnish evidence of their compliance. For this purpose, it has exhorted them to keep a record of their attendances at courses and their participation in other approved activities. At the time this chapter was written the initial year of the scheme's operation had recently concluded and the Law Society was engaged in processing solicitors' applications for the renewal of their practising certificates. Presumably, the Board will shortly refer the first batch of defaulting solicitors to the Society for disciplinary action.

There has been a wide spectrum of opinion about Mandatory CLE amongst the ranks of the profession. It has ranged from enthusiastic support to expressions of outraged opposition, particularly from older practitioners. This vigorous debate was reflected in the *Law Society Journal* (the solicitors' professional journal) over the period of 12 months prior to the implementation of the scheme. Now that it has been running for a year opinions may well have been tempered, with some who formerly opposed the scheme now recognising that there are benefits to be gained. However, there is probably still a rump of grudging acquiescence, which must impact upon the motivation to learn.

Despite its commitment to the principle of Mandatory CLE, the Law Society has not produced a policy document as such. The Mandatory CLE Board has distributed to all solicitors a booklet entitled *The Practitioners' Guide to Mandatory Continuing Legal Education in New South Wales*. However, this merely explains how the scheme is intended to operate and not the rationale for the adoption of Mandatory CLE as a policy. Presumably, it is to the Fox Report (Law Society of New South Wales, 1985) and to statements in the *Law Society Journal* that one should go in order to discover the Society's reasoning. When one does so, it becomes apparent that the Society has turned to Mandatory CLE in the belief that it will ensure a minimum level of competence within the profession. The Society has responded to an emerging consumerism, deriving from a heightened public and government dissatisfaction with the quality of the services offered by professionals.

However, in doing so, it appears to have neglected to address the educational considerations inherent in mandatory CPE. The Fox Report, which provided the background information upon which its decision was based, deals cursorily with the considerable body of literature generated by the debate about mandatory education for professionals. This literature reveals that there is no empirical evidence to support the proposition that mandatory CPE schemes make a direct contribution to improved competence. The only behaviour they require is attendance, which does not guarantee that any learning has taken place. They make no attempt to evaluate changes in knowledge or professional performance resulting from participation. Indeed, this point was conceded in the admission in the Fox Report that, while the other desired benefits might not accrue, at the very least the scheme it proposed should have the effect of forcing practitioners to address the question of their educational needs. Furthermore, mandatory CPE schemes, while providing the motivation to attend, may be detrimental to learning taking place, due to the resentment and hostility generated in some participants.

It would also appear that in the planning stages the Law Society neither referred to the literature and research on adult learning principles nor consulted anyone with acknowledged expertise in adult and continuing education. Had it done so, it would have appreciated that adults have different learning styles, which result in their learning in diverse ways. By imposing uniformity in this respect, mandatory CPE schemes fail to recognise that there are other roads to professional competence, such as private study. In omitting credit for them, there is a danger that these other valid modes of increasing competence will be downgraded and discouraged. The issues in the debate about mandatory CPE are far more complex than this brief review suggests and very much beyond the scope of this profile (for example, see Nelson, 1988).

The Law Society could well have targeted several priority groups within the profession. One would assume that some sections, such as sole practitioners, those from remote areas of the state and newly admitted solicitors would be at most risk professionally and would therefore have a greater need for CPE than others. However, the Mandatory CLE scheme imposes the same requirement upon all members of the profession without regard to these sorts of factors.

The management of CLE

The Mandatory CLE Board is responsible for administering the scheme on behalf of the Law Society. The Board's principal function is the accreditation of the educational activities of specific providers which, in its judgment, satisfy certain criteria. Providers are required to demonstrate that their programs are of 'significant intellectual or practical merit', deal primarily with matters directly related to the practice of law and are taught by 'persons who are qualified by practical or academic experience in the subjects covered' (Mandatory CLE Board, 1987). The Board also determines the number of CLE units to be granted for each accredited program, as well as giving credit to individual solicitors for presentations given, articles written or attendances at non-accredited courses. It has the power, in exceptional circumstances, to grant conditional, partial or complete exemption from the prescribed requirements, which power has been exercised, for example, in the case of a small number of senior practitioners. It is responsible for recommending to the Society that disciplinary action, including the suspension or cancellation of practising certificates, be taken against defaulters. Although not specifically stated, it also has the duty to disseminate information to solicitors and providers about the functioning of the scheme. The experience gained during the first 12 months of the scheme's operation has resulted in the development of a body of rulings, especially in the area of accreditation, which the Board now applies.

The Board is composed of ten members, at least seven of whom must be practising solicitors. An effort has been made to reflect the total profile of the profession by including corporate and government lawyers, as well as solicitors in private practice. In order to give the appropriate educational input, an academic lawyer, the head of the College of Law's

THE LEGAL PROFESSION 59

CLE Department and a lay member with a background in education also sit on the Board. The members are appointed by the President of the Law Society.

Because there are many different categories of CLE providers, the Mandatory CLE Board can only manage the scheme at the front end. The criteria for accreditation which it applies are very general. If it appears on the face of a provider's application that a proposed activity meets those criteria, then it will be accredited. Reliance seems to be placed on its perceptions of the reputation of the provider and the professional qualifications and experience of the presenter. Less stress is placed upon educational considerations; for example, whether the particular activity reflects the overall objectives of the scheme in improving competence levels within the profession, whether the presenter is suitably qualified as a teacher (as opposed to a lawyer) and whether the delivery system is appropriate for the nature of the subject matter and the level at which the activity is pitched. No attempt is made to monitor the quality of programs after they have been held or to assess their impact upon professional performance, which would admittedly be difficult with the sheer variety of offerings. Moreover, the Board does not appear to have been assigned a role in coordinating the activities of all providers. It does have a duty to report to the Society any significant deficiencies in the availability of CLE, but only in relation to whether there are sufficient activities on offer to enable solicitors to gain their ten CLE units each year (Mandatory CLE Board, 1987). Because of the range of providers and activities and the fact that the obligation is imposed uniformly upon all members, there is no real possibility that CPE could become a central controlling function in the legal profession.

Program content and delivery

There is no overall Mandatory CLE program, as the scheme relies on individual providers to decide upon the activities they should offer, before having them accredited by the Board. The topics for new activities are generated in a variety of ways. For example, the Head of the CLE Department of the College of Law has indicated that its activities evolve from a 'grab-bag of ideas' collected over time. These include suggestions from practitioners and the Law Society committees, articles in the press and legal journals and the advertising brochures of other providers. Moreover, the College has standing consultative committees in various areas of legal practice, which keep it alert to new developments. From time to time a need arises to find a place in the program for courses on 'hot topics'. These are intended to react to major changes in the law, which are shortly to come into effect and which will impact significantly upon standard practice. For example, the anti-gazumping legislation recently introduced in New South Wales made fundamental changes to conveyancing practice. The College's response was to run a series of courses on this topic at venues in the city of Sydney, the suburbs and the country to provide maximum exposure to the large number of solicitors whose practices were affected by this new law. At the other end of the spectrum, the need is also recognised for comprehensive courses on more settled areas of law and practice pitched at a fundamental level. These are intended to assist those who need to bring themselves up-to-date, as well as to help those who have never practised in the area but who plan to do so in the future. They should be of particular value to those solicitors whose regular areas of practice have contracted due to legislative change.

Neither the College of Law nor other providers has attempted to assess the learning needs of solicitors across the profession, as part of the process of program development. For those in charge of the in-house CLE programs in the law firms, government departments and corporations, as well as the special interest groups, it is much easier to identify the needs of their clientele. They are more accessible and they practise in readily defined areas. On the other hand, the larger providers who aim to serve the whole profession probably do not recognise the uses to which information on educational needs can be put when they develop their programs. They may also be distrustful of a data-gathering procedure which they see as difficult to design, expensive to administer and yielding a wealth of information which may be hard to reduce to useable form.

The range of topics offered by the CLE providers is very wide. It reflects the diversity of the practice of law which intrudes into so many aspects of community life. These topics might be classified under general headings which relate to traditional sub-divisions of law, such as commercial law, family law, criminal law, conveyancing, administration of estates and will drafting. CLE also includes activities designed to enhance the legal skills which solicitors need to employ in conducting their practices, such as advocacy, negotiating, interviewing, drafting and researching skills. Courses on various aspects of office and practice management are popular, particularly those which deal with computer useage in the legal office. There have been occasional cross-disciplinary activities, for example accountancy for lawyers and medicine and the law. The small number of courses relating to aspects of human resources development have attracted the most criticism. For example, there was an outcry from various sections of the profession when a course on stress management offered by the College of Law was accredited by the Mandatory CLE Board. The argument was that this topic did not fall within the ambit of the criteria for CLE activities.

With 10,000 solicitors falling within the ambit of the Mandatory CLE scheme, it is self-evident that the opportunities for providers have expanded greatly under Mandatory CLE. It is now big business and can be very lucrative. Under voluntary CLE the College of Law was probably responsible for in excess of two-thirds of the offerings. Even with the increase in its activities which Mandatory CLE has entailed, it is doubtful whether the College of Law has maintained that same share of the augmented market. However, it is still by far the largest single provider. The other traditional providers of voluntary CLE who are still actively engaged are the universities, the regional law societies in the suburbs and the country, and the Young Lawyers' Section of the Law Society. However, in the wake of Mandatory CLE, new providers have entered the field. These include the bulk of the commercial providers, although some, such as the Business Law Education Centre (BLEC), were active well before CLE became mandatory. They tend to cater primarily for members of the larger city law firms, which can more readily afford their fees. However, several of these large Sydney firms have also established their own in-house CLE. Recently a few have appointed educational directors to run their programs and, in some cases, to promote the professional development of the solicitors on their staff. Similarly, the legal sections of a number of government departments and corporations have had their own in-house CLE programs accredited under the scheme. For those working within narrow specialties, the opportunity is available to set up their own special interest groups and to conduct CLE activities tailored to their members' particular needs.

It would seem that CPE presenters are a mixed lot. They are often other solicitors or barristers who are acknowledged experts in the area. Sometimes judges or magistrates are involved. For the more fundamental courses they are frequently drawn from the instructors in the College of Law's practical legal training course. Occasionally, presenters are from different professions, such as accountants, surveyors or psychologists. Although they may be the content experts, they are sometimes deficient in the delivery of that content. The need to give attention to training the presenters to develop better instructional skills and employ alternative teaching techniques is slowly being accepted.

As to *delivery systems*, lectures still tend to be the usual format. With the large numbers attending the more popular activities and the fact that many presenters are untrained in alternative teaching strategies, this prevalence of lectures is inevitable. Some attempt is made to achieve interaction between presenters and participants by having question and answer sessions at the conclusion of each session. There is a growing use of audio-visual aids, especially overhead projectors. More student-centred teaching methods are emerging, such as small group discussions, workshops, case studies and role plays. There is some recognition that different strategies may be appropriate for activities pitched at different levels. For example, with a fundamental course on an established area where the concern is to ensure that participants have acquired the basic essentials for competent practice, small group discussions or workshops might be more effective. On the other hand, with the reactive courses dealing with recent changes in practice, the emphasis will be upon conveying the necessary knowledge quickly. Here the lecture probably remains the most suitable method of delivery.

There is a growing range of videotape and audiocasette material being produced on legal topics, which satisfies the accreditation criteria. Despite their value to remote practitioners, they probably tend to be used more in the larger metropolitan law firms. One consideration is the cost of hiring or buying the tapes, which is more economical for the bigger firms; another is that if the showing of the video is accompanied by commentary from a suitably qualified and experienced video commentator participation counts for more CLE units. The College of Law has produced a small number of self-contained training packages incorporating videotape instruction with written materials and exercises. The Business Law Education Centre offers a subscription service to a monthly legal update presented by video. However, other more sophisticated distance education modes, such as video- and tele-conferencing have not been exploited, largely because they appear to be less economical than what is presently offered. The needs of country practitioners are mainly met by the College of Law which uses several regional centres with good quality seminar, accommodation and transport facilities. These serve as catchment areas for solicitors in the surrounding localities. Sufficient CLE activities are offered each year at these venues to enable participants to accumulate their required ten CLE units.

Evaluation

There is an element of accountability through the accreditation procedures to the Mandatory CLE Board acting on behalf of the Law Society. With such a large range of activities on offer and varying fee levels, the market place provides some vetting of quality. However, the Board does not seek to gauge the success of individual activities after they have been conducted; that is left to the individual providers. In the case of the College of Law, participants are requested to complete an evaluation sheet at the conclusion of each session. They are asked what they liked and disliked and to provide suggestions for improvement and propose topics for related courses. The evaluation is neither merely a 'happiness indicator' nor a public relations exercise. A report is compiled on each activity for the benefit of repeat sessions and sent to the presenter with comments as to how the presentation could have been improved.

At the macro-level, there has been no attempt to determine the success of Mandatory CLE as a whole. Of course, it is early days yet. However, consideration will need to be given in the near future to assessing the impact which the mandatory scheme has made upon improving the standards of competence and performance across the profession. There is no justification for simply presuming that this whole Mandatory CLE enterprise, which is so costly in terms of time, energy and money, has achieved its objectives.

Mandatory CPE schemes leave a lingering doubt as to whether the primary concern of the sponsoring professional association is really continuing education. Its purpose may be to offer some guarantee to the public and to government by recertifying its members as competent to practise, in order to preserve its privilege of self-regulation (Nelson, 1988). While this must be an element in any profession's decision to introduce mandatory CPE, there is no clear evidence that this was a strong motivation behind the Law Society's Mandatory CLE scheme. There does appear to be a genuine concern to enhance competence and performance within the profession and there is no overt attempt to exploit the fact that CLE is mandatory for the purpose of public relations.

The Board does not monitor attendance. Providers are required to keep attendance records for each of their activities but these are of limited value and, in effect, an honour system prevails. The Law Society obviously considers that the penalties which attach to completing a false declaration when applying to renew a practising certificate, along with the risk of being selected at random to produce evidence of compliance, are a sufficient deterrent to those who might be tempted to cheat on the scheme.

Finance

Except in the case of some in-house CLE, the Mandatory CLE scheme functions on the user-pays principle. Accordingly, the fees that are set for each of the activities are intended to cover all operating expenses. Several of the providers would be content so long as they did not incur a loss and would be largely unconcerned about profit. On the other hand, those who are engaged in CLE for commercial reasons would probably set their fees at a higher level in order to attain a preset profit margin. One considerable advantage flowing from Mandatory CLE for the College of Law, as the largest provider, is that there is now less need to fret when individual activities are poorly attended, because economies of scale come into play overall. Fortunately, there is no flow-on relating to the costs of running the Mandatory CLE Board itself: its operating expenses are presently covered by the interest earned on a capital grant from a fund administered by the Law Society.

There is some evidence that the high costs of a small number of the activities are a barrier to participation for some solicitors. However, under the scheme there is so much choice and providers generally appear to be making efforts to keep costs down, so this would appear to be a fairly insignificant element.

Likely future developments

Amongst the probable developments are an increase in the number of solicitors who will acquire their CLE through in-house programs, particularly in the bigger city law firms. As a result, the College of Law may well find that the focal point of its market has shifted to the smaller law firms in the suburbs of Sydney and the country. More specialist groups are likely to be formed to cater for the needs of those who are out of the mainstream of practice. There may also be more courses dealing with basic areas of practice and more workshop-based activities extending over periods of half a day or a day.

At the time of writing, the Mandatory CLE scheme has been in operation for just over a year, so it is too early to assess the impact which it has had upon enhancing competence and performance levels within the legal profession. During this period the main emphasis has been upon establishing the scheme. Providers have had to take a short-term view and concentrate upon gearing up for the major expansion in their activities which Mandatory CLE has entailed. When the dust settles, it will be possible to look beyond the immediate concerns. However, in my opinion, one problem area which is already apparent relates to the lack of an overall educational program tailored to the objectives of the scheme. Provision tends to be fragmentary and uncoordinated. There are as many CLE programs as there are providers. It is these providers, not the Mandatory CLE Board nor the Law Society, which determine what activities will be offered to solicitors. Moreover, the quality mechanism is rudimentary. It is only at the proposal stage that any monitoring is carried out by the Board and this appears to be educationally unsophisticated. Activities are not evaluated after they have been conducted. It seems to be presumed that the mere existence of competition between providers for the CLE dollar will guarantee quality. No record is maintained by the Board of the success or failure of activities so as to avoid repeating the same mistakes.

And yet the groundswell of opposition within the profession appears to have substantially moderated over this period. The experience of having participated in the activities offered under the scheme seems to have persuaded many that it can make a powerful contribution towards meeting their educational needs and strengthening their performance as practitioners. If the scheme is to capitalise on this improved image, it must devise more effective mechanisms to assure the quality of the programs offered under the banner of Mandatory CLE.

References

Bennett, J. M. (1984). *A history of solicitors in New South Wales.* Sydney: Legal Books Pty Limited.

Brennan, B. (1988). Challenges to continuing professional education in Australia. In D. R. Dymock, (ed.), *Continuing professional education — policy and provision.* Armidale: University of New England, Dept of Continuing Education.

Edwards, M. F. (1985). Mandatory CLE: Shield or sham? *Journal of Professional Legal Education* 3(1), 65–78.

Fox Report. *See* Law Society of New South Wales. (1985).

Law Society of New South Wales. (Chairman: Fox). (1985). *Report of the law reform committee on mandatory continuing legal education.* Sydney, NSW: author.

Mackay. D. G. (1981). Strategies for continuing legal education. In J. Bowen & C. Mitchelmore, (eds), *Continuing legal education in the 1980s.* Sydney: Law Foundation of New South Wales.

Mandatory Continuing Legal Education Board (1987). *The practitioners' guide to mandatory continuing legal education in New South Wales.* Sydney, NSW: author.

Nelson, J. W. (1988). Program design and delivery under mandatory continuing professional education. *Studies in Continuing Education,* 10(2), 81–103.

Riches, A. L. N. (1988). Continuing judicial education in New South Wales. *Journal of Professional Legal Education,* 6(2), 150–162.

Schein, E. H. (1972). *Professional education: Some new directions.* New York: McGraw-Hill Book Company.

5
The Accounting Profession

DALJIT SINGH

Contextual factors

There are two major professional accounting bodies in Australia: the Australian Society of Accountants (ASA) and the Institute of Chartered Accountants in Australia (ICA). The ASA was formed in 1952 although some of its antecedent bodies came into existence in 1886. The ICA was formed in 1928, following the grant of a Royal Charter; some of its antecedent bodies had been in existence since 1885. For a comparative historical perspective, the Institute of Chartered Accountants in England and Wales commenced in 1880 (Farrell, 1986).

In 1987, the ICA had 16,300 members (ICA, 1987) whereas the ASA had 54,300 members (ASA, 1987), making the latter the third-largest accounting body in the world. Women comprised 8 per cent of the ICA membership and 12 per cent of the ASA. In terms of composition of membership by field of employment, the ICA had a majority of its members in public practice (57 per cent in 1987) compared to the ASA (22 per cent in 1987) while the ASA had a larger proportion of its members (70 per cent) employed in commerce, industry, government and so on than the ICA's 43 per cent. The difference in membership distribution by field of employment is largely due to the differences in membership admission criteria of the two bodies. These differences do go some way to explaining the differences in their approaches to CPE.

The ICA's basic entry requirements, (for Associate membership) are:

1. an approved tertiary degree;
2. completion of the Professional Year of Study (PY) administered by the Institute, as a series of examinable modules, taken only by candidates in the employment of a Chartered Accountant in public practice; and
3. completion of at least three years of practical experience in the office of a Chartered Accountant in public practice.

The ASA's basic entry requirements (for Associate membership) are:

1. an approved tertiary degree;
2. completion of the Associate program, administered by the Society, which involves one examinable module; and
3. completion of the required period of experience (three years supervised or five years unsupervised by a member of the ASA or ICA).

It should be noted that the ICA requirement of completion of experience in 'public practice' is in sharp contrast to the ASA requirement, which does not specify the field of employment. The ICA entry rules effectively exclude accountants employed in commerce, government, or academia as those fields are not considered to be public practice. However, on attaining ICA membership, members can elect to leave public practice and join other fields of employment, while still retaining their ICA membership. There are instances of dual membership of both bodies, although it is difficult to obtain verifiable figures of the extent.

There have been two major attempts at unifying the two accounting bodies (in 1969 and 1981) but on both occasions, they failed due to the inability to secure the required assenting votes from the ICA membership. The two bodies maintain close links, especially in regard to technical accounting issues (issuing joint technical standards through a jointly sponsored Australian Accounting Research Foundation) and in joint submissions to government and Commissions of Inquiry. There is support within the executives of both bodies and among many senior members of the profession for the integration of the ASA and the ICA. This support has had an indirect impact on CPE policies. It should be noted here that the two organisations use different terminology. The ICA refers to 'continuing professional education' (CPE), while the ASA prefers 'continuing professional development' (CPD), or simply 'professional development' (PD).

Policy and objectives

The Australian Society of Accountants

The ASA held its first 'professional development' labelled activity in 1968, (McKeon, 1978) and the ICA held its first such activity in 1967 (Graham, 1978). By the late 1970s both bodies had begun to consider CPE seriously, recommending it to their members.

In 1980 the ASA commenced a scheme of 'voluntary' reporting by members of CPE activities, with a recommendation of a minimum of 120 hours per triennium. Members were required to report annually if they wished to participate and a certificate of compliance was to be issued at the end of the triennium. The response to the program of voluntary compliance was poor and in 1983, after the end of the first triennium, an ASA task force on CPE stated that it expected less than 5 per cent of the total membership to receive certificates of compliance (Pryor, 1983). However, debate had occurred within the profession on the mandatory versus voluntary issue in the 1970s. For example, within the ASA, the Professional Development Officer in 1972 discussed the importance of CPE for the profession including the trend overseas towards compulsory CPE (Russell, 1972). He also noted (Russell, 1973) that the threat of government regulation existed if the profession were to fail to act on setting a 'suitable' CPE policy. He used overseas models of CPE, particularly from the United States, as examples of the need for compulsory professional development.

An ASA member replied critically to Russell's articles, suggesting that the ASA's CPE concept to date was based on misdirected ideas and a misconception of the needs of the body of members (McLean, 1974). Russell, of the ASA, raised the issue again in 1976, in an article entitled 'Compulsory Professional Development: Yes or No?' in the ASA journal *Australian Accountant* (see Russell, 1976). He was by then 'Director' of PD rather than 'officer', signifying the increased stature the function had acquired by the mid-1970s. He asked accountants to remember that the *trend* to compulsory CPE had been noticeable in other professions as well as overseas and:

> not to ignore one of the lessons of history. Namely, that once a trend has been set in motion, rarely is it reversed. Thus, perhaps we should devote our energies to deciding 'when?' and 'how?' rather than 'should?'. (Russell, 1976, p. 279).

In 1978 Russell's successor as Director (Cook) discussed members' reactions to the concept of compulsory professional development. Of 53 written responses to the PD question, the numbers for and against compulsion were equal (17) while the 'fence-sitters' totalled 19 persons (Cook, 1978). Arguments advanced through this survey *for* compulsion included the importance of maintaining competence and the need to take action before government regulation occurred etc. Arguments advanced *against* included the arguments that members knew what was best for them and that competence standards were already high.

By 1980 it appeared that the ASA had 'formally' decided that CPE was appropriate and instituted the voluntary compliance. The poor response to this move was apparent by the end of the triennium ending December 1982. A CPD Task Force of the ASA developed a response entitled 'The Professional Schedule', which was unveiled in 1983 (Pryor, 1983). The Schedule acknowledged that CPD was a 'principal reason' for the existence of a professional body. The ASA invited comments from ASA members and it also commissioned outside professional surveys to obtain informed comment from the members of the ASA, financial controllers of the largest 100 companies in Australia, and accounting students. After studying these comments, the ASA judged that there was sufficient support for the Schedule and adopted it in 1983, with a transitional phase in 1984 and an 'effective' phase commencing 1 January 1985. The mandatory CPE obligations relating to the Schedule are provided in Table 5.1.

The Schedule also introduced a form of membership distinct from that held by previous members (AASA). This new membership was the CPA (Certified Practising Accountant). The CPA was projected by the ASA to signify the highest level of membership in the profession and synonymous with professionalism. As shown in Table 5.1, CPAs are expected to commit themselves to at least 60 hours of compulsory CPE per triennium. Under the transitional requirements, existing ASA members were allowed to automatically 'transfer' from AASA to CPA, provided membership had been held for at least two years and many elected to do so. The CPA designation also requires the passing of several modular examinations. The AASA designation was retained as a lower level of membership, with no obligation to attend CPE activities. The ASA also decided to terminate the voluntary CPE 'certificate of compliance' scheme by 1989. The ASA also introduced 'specialist' member status

Table 5.1 Summary of CPE Obligations for Members of the Australian Society of Accountants

Member status	Obligations	Annual reporting required
Provisional Associate	Nil (voluntary)	No
Associate (AASA)	Nil (voluntary)	No
Certified Practising Accountant (AASA CPA)	60 hours per triennium	No
CPA or AASA Senior with one specialisation or more	120 hours per triennium, including not less than 60 specialist hours 60 hours for any other additional specialisations (for example, 180 hours total for two specialisations)	Yes
Public Practice Certificate Holder	120 hours per triennium, including not less than 60 hours of 'structured' activities	Yes
Public Practice Certificate Holder with one specialisation or more	120 hours per triennium, including not less than 60 hours of 'structured' activities and not less than 60 hours in specialisation held (for example, 180 hours total if two specialisations are held)	Yes

where a CPA could elect to specialise in one of the following fields: Auditing, External Reporting, Insolvency and Reconstruction, Management Accounting, and Taxation and Treasury. The specialisation designation carried an increased obligation to CPE. For example, to have one field of specialisation with CPA required a minimum of 120 hours of CPE per triennium with at least 60 hours of CPE per triennium to be in the specialisation field (see Table 5.1).

The ASA followed the launching of the Professional Schedule with a concentrated television advertising campaign on the CPA, with the theme 'Not Your Average Accountant'. It has generally been recognised within the profession that the ASA was aiming to lift the profile of its membership and also compete with the ICA's prestigious membership designation of 'Chartered Accountant'. The ASA appears eager for integration with the ICA and various public utterances by ASA officials (presidents, etc.) and ASA journal statements also readily acknowledge this. (See for example, the article entitled 'The CPA — An Appreciating Asset' in the *Australian Accountant*, March 1988, (pp. 19–22).)

A reading of the Professional Schedule enables the following objectives of CPE to be discerned. The objectives are based on the Society's recognition that there are two pillars of professionalism — competence and integrity — and that CPE is a principal basis for the existence of a 'professional' body. As the CPA designation is the mark of high professional competence, competence must be maintained by a commitment to CPE by CPAs.

The Institute of Chartered Accountants

The year 1985 was also a landmark one for the ICA, which introduced in July of that year the concept of compulsory CPE for ICA members. In 1979, the Institute had issued a recommendation that all members undertake a minimum of 120 hours of CPE activity per triennium. Presumably, the result was disappointing, as with the ASA, leading to mandatory CPE in 1985. The National Professional Development Committee and the National Professional Standards Committee of the ICA together with the ICA National Council influenced the formation of the CPE policy. As with the ASA, overseas trends towards compulsory CPE were an important influence. The ICA's policy on CPE was issued in 1985 and is contained in the ICA *Members' Handbook* (1987).

> A member has a duty to maintain his level of competence throughout his professional career. He must only undertake work which he or his firm can expect to complete with professional competence.

The obligation to undertake CPE can be linked to that statement which is similar in intent to the ASA's CPE policy objectives, that is, the maintenance of technical competence. Both bodies also have a message to the public and government through their CPE policy, namely, that

THE ACCOUNTING PROFESSION 73

they take a *professional stance* on the matter of maintaining and improving standards of competence of their members. The ICA requirement is for members to undertake a minimum of 40 hours of CPE per annum, of which at least 20 hours must be 'structured' CPE. Table 5.2 (page 74) lists the activities that count for CPE for both the ASA and the ICA, including which activities are considered to be structured and unstructured. For the ASA, it is only for the Public Practice Certificate category of membership that any minimum amount of 'structured' CPE activity is required (see Table 5.1). This implies a more stringent CPE rule in terms of the structured minimum hours by the ICA compared to the ASA. Furthermore, the ICA rules apply uniformly to its membership while the Associate members of the ASA (below CPA) have no obligation to commit themselves to CPE. One could ask *how professional* is the AASA designation, in view of the linking of CPE to the maintenance of professional competence by the ASA (for example, the CPA designation).

Management

At the national level, CPE activity is managed by the Director of Professional Development in the ASA and the Director of Education and Professional Development in the ICA. There are only four and five directorships at the national level of the ASA and ICA respectively, thus indicating that CPE is an important function. However, CPE is not the only function of PD directors; they may have additional responsibilities relating to the initial training of accountants.

Both bodies have National Committees for Professional Development which have an influence on CPE policy. However, the National Councils of both bodies determine and issue CPE policy. The National PD Committees act as important sources of coordination and information flow regarding CPE and work closely with state PD committees. These committees have a mixture of appointed and co-opted members with a selective use of 'outsiders' such as academics. The ASA also has assistant PD directors in several states. The annual reports of both the ICA and ASA give state-by-state coverage of CPE activity, signifying the role CPE has in the profession. CPE provision appears to be decentralised so that the states can assess their own unique markets and provide CPE courses at state level.

Table 5.2 Comparison of Acceptable CPE Activities — ASA and ICA

CPE activity	ASA	ICA
Structured		
Congresses, conventions by a professional accounting body	✓ No restriction to type of session	✓ Restriction to technical sessions only
Courses, seminars, workshops and other PD activities presented by a professional accounting body	✓	✓
Discussion groups	✓ If under ASA aegis only	✓ No restriction; can be other bodies
In-house courses (member's employer)	✓	✓
Tertiary courses by educational institutes (aside from those required for membership purposes)	✓	✓
CPE activities by other organisations	✓	✓
Research, writing and presenting technical material	✓	✓
Service on technical or research committees of professional accounting bodies or other bodies	✓	✓
Programmed self-study	✓	✓
Unstructured		
Individual study, informal discussion and study groups	✓	✓

The rationale for the management structure for both bodies is that CPE activity occurs at the state level and so active management is appropriate at that level. At the national level, there is coordination of activity, flow of information and the provision of an advisory service and policy input function. State PD Committee input to national CPE policy is also important because of the present management structure of CPE in the profession.

Program content and delivery

The overall program for CPE for both the ASA and ICA consists of the separate CPE components of the various states. Each state determines their own CPE based on their assessment of the needs of members and with the support and assistance of the national level of CPE when necessary. The needs assessment has occasionally used survey instruments. A wide range of topics is covered from technical topics such as tax, accounting requirements of the Companies Code and budgeting to management topics such as effective communication at work, meeting management and negotiating skills. The lecture is the dominant means of presentation, although increasing use is being made of workshops, discussion groups, seminars and case studies utilising technology such as videos and computers. Continuing professional education activity also includes audio-tape and video-tape services, utilising services supplied by the accounting bodies as well as outside organisations. Computer-based learning is also evident in some ASA courses. Distance education is already being used by the ASA in its CPA examinable module series and it is expected that this mode will be extended to other CPE activities in the future.

Program delivery personnel include a wide range of individuals and organisations. They include chartered accountants, marketing and management specialists and computer specialists. There are also some in-house presenters who have administrative and marketing backgrounds. The ASA and the ICA also conduct a range of joint-CPE activities. In the Australian Capital Territory, there is even a joint PD committee and several joint activities there are conducted by both bodies.

There is also a close degree of cooperation between some tertiary institutions and the professional bodies on CPE activities. Joint courses have also been run in conjunction with some government departments, for example, seminars on New South Wales state tax updates have been presented by the Department of Finance jointly for the ASA, ICA and the Law Society of New South Wales. International visitors have also been speakers at CPE activities organised by the ASA and ICA. Regular monthly newsletters by the bodies in every state provide information on the variety of CPE activities available.

Future likely developments in program content and delivery include a greater diversity of delivery modes and presenters, with even more extensive use of technology such as satellite conferences and interactive videos. In 1987 the ASA held its first satellite conference, on the theme of 'Legislative Changes to Superannuation', which was beamed live from Sydney to audiences in other state capitals.

Evaluation

The provision of CPE is accountable through the state committees to the respective state councils and then to the national committees and through the National Directors to the National Councils of the respective bodies. Accountability embraces both the programming and financial aspects as for both the ICA and ASA, CPE is run on the *user-pays* principle. There is a proviso that the needs of members must be balanced with commercial pressures. For the ICA there is some evidence to suggest that some country area CPE activity is being subsidised by capital city CPE activity (Poole, 1987).

The success of individual activities is gauged in two ways: comments of participants and the number of attendees. The program does not offer any guarantees as such to attendees. Evaluation instruments (questionnaire-based) are used for each activity with questions on competence and quality control in regard to presenters, content matter and other aspects of organisation such as venue and timing. Attendances of members are recorded individually by members as both ASA and ICA members need to keep records of CPE activities as they can be asked to produce evidence of CPE participation. Registers of attendance are also kept for all CPE activities by the ASA and ICA.

The failure or success of CPE activities appears to be determined on two criteria: the degree of satisfaction of participants and the number of attendees (and therefore financial performance). In the author's view, while input measures (resources applied and CPE hours recorded) may be established, concern has to be raised about output measures (results). As CPE is concerned with maintaining and improving competence levels, *measurement* of competence is a desirable, although difficult, task that the profession must examine more closely. Furthermore, needs assessment methods require re-examination. The assessment of members' needs by both bodies are based on the opinions of panels and committees, aided by occasional surveys. This process tends to produce lists of what some members *want* rather than what they *need*. This point has also been made by Birkett (1980, pp. 3–4):

> The difficulty is that opinions of accountants about their needs are likely to be fragmentary and reflect their experience and conditioning more than their changing needs; and the responses of accountants to surveys of their needs are likely to reflect the set of opinions embodied in the survey instruments, which reflect in turn the experience and conditioning of the members of the profession who conduct the survey. The result is a 'closed' system about continuing education needs, one that can change slowly, and one that may not represent the needs that exist. Some research designed to gather new evidence about the work, tasks, career paths and profiles of accountants as these relate to continuing education needs would seem to be warranted, given the substantial effort and expense that is being devoted to the 'continuing education of accountants' or that is being proposed.

Birkett also noted that there is no assessment of the 'quality' of the compliance, that mere compliance is sufficient; nor is there any assessment of the 'gains' made as a result of compliance. His comments indicate the need for more research on the *competence measurement* of accountants with its implications for CPE. If this is accepted as desirable, 'competence' itself would need to be defined and appropriate measurement devices developed. Birkett (1980) provides a useful start in this direction through a model which explores the relationships between the nature of accounting work, tasks, career profiles, professional competence, skills and capacities and links these to CPE needs, which result in CPE processes (institutional location and bases for learning strategies).

The present CPE program remains technically oriented for both the ASA and ICA. Perhaps this is a result of present needs assessment procedures being based on what accountants appear to want rather than what they need. Miller's comments, that few CPE activities appear to

78 CONTINUING PROFESSIONAL EDUCATION

meet the needs of members to improve their performance as managers whether in practice or in industry (Miller, 1979), still appear to apply.

Finance

It has been noted earlier that both the ASA and ICA operate CPE on a *user-pays* principle and that, for the ASA, mandatory CPE for some designations of membership came into effect on 1 January 1985 while for the ICA it was from 1 July 1985. Table 5.3 provides a comparison of the revenue received and expenditure incurred for CPE by the two bodies in 1985 and 1987, highlighting the growth of CPE in dollar terms. For the ASA, CPE revenue as a percentage of total revenue was 9 per cent in 1985 and 10 per cent in 1987. For the ICA comparable figures are 9 per cent and 12 per cent (1985 and 1987 respectively). It is interesting to note that the ASA recorded a smaller percentage increase in CPE revenues between 1985 and 1987 than did the ICA. This could perhaps be attributed to the minimum of 20 hours per annum mandatory CPE for CPAs not having a minimum structured element while there is a minimum 20 hours per annum structured element of the total CPE requirement for ICA members. This policy could have resulted in some ASA members having less incentive to attend ASA formal CPE activities and opting for more unstructured activities.

At least $3 million is spent annually on professionally organised CPE activities by both bodies (see Table 5.3). In addition, both bodies have approved a large number of other activities as 'CPE' (see Table 5.2). The financial expenditure by members is therefore likely to be very much higher. For instance, the 'Big Eight' accounting firms in Australia (which are part of the eight largest international firms of accountants in the world) have extensive training programs, many elements of which would qualify as CPE activity and these alone would run into several millions of dollars per annum.

Sponsorship of CPE does take place. Although it is difficult to obtain precise figures, sponsorship is probably more than one-quarter of a million dollars per annum for the profession. While it has generally been accepted that cost is not a particular barrier to participation, there has been some disquiet amongst some rural members of the profession that CPE courses are too expensive, because of the smaller numbers at rural

Table 5.3 Comparison of CPE Revenues and Expenditures of ASA and ICA, 1985 and 1987

	1985	1987	Increase
	($ 000)		(%)
ASA			
CPE revenue	1285	1946	51
CPE expenditure	1494	1947	30
Surplus (loss)	(209)	(1)	
ICA			
CPE revenue	635	1274	100
CPE expenditure	568	965	69
Surplus (loss)	67	309	

Source: *ASA Annual Reports*, 1985 and 1987; and *ICA Annual Reports*, 1985 and 1987.

centres. This problem is being overcome by giving rural members the opportunity to attend CPE activities in one session. For example, the week-long 'Update Series' run by the Darling Downs Institute of Advanced Education in Queensland enables a member to fully comply with CPE requirements.

Likely future developments

By the mid-1980s both the ICA and the ASA had mechanisms in place for mandatory CPE thus indicating the importance of CPE to the profession. The CPE issue as members see it today involves not only the issue of maintaining individual competence of members but also conveying the professionalism of accountants to major interest groups such as consumers of accounting services, accounting regulators, the general public and government. This CPE strategy recognises that the only basis for claiming professionalism is one of knowledge (Matthews, 1981).

The *defence* of professionalism via mandatory CPE against further government regulation has already been evident overseas, for example in the USA (Buckley & Weston, 1980). In Australia, where 'public registration' of accountants is only required in two states (New South

Wales and Queensland), the need for the profession to convey this *message of professionalism* is also equally important. The strategy also recognises the challenges being faced by the professions generally where long-held traditions and beliefs are under question (Kirby, 1980).

A major issue for accountants in the future relates to the unification of the two bodies, the ASA and the ICA. This will have direct implications for CPE as policy prescriptions differ depending on designation of membership (especially with the various levels of membership within the ASA). The question also arises as to how the 'specialisation' designation (with CPE commitments to specialisation) adopted by the ASA, would fare in a merger. A possible rationalisation of CPE resources would be of great benefit to professional accountants. It is the belief of the author that the merger will ultimately take place, although it could be a few years away as both bodies are cautious after the two previous failed attempts. The marketing of the CPA designation and its related CPE commitment could play a role in persuading ICA members (the major stumbling block in the past) that a merger will not detract from the perceived prestige of the membership of the Institute. Further, the profession is concerned that currently about 22 per cent of graduates do not join either accounting body. A past president of the ASA (Wright, 1986) has stated that graduates need to be convinced that the bodies are seen and known to be vibrant professional bodies, actively servicing and promoting their members to be first class professionals. These comments have implications for the role of CPE in the profession.

Other likely developments include the growing sophistication of both bodies in analysing the needs of their members and in adopting more refined evaluation instruments to judge the quality and effects of their CPE activities. This development will be assisted by increasing experience of CPE management, programming and evaluation. It is also likely that there will be more extensive use of high technology tools, such as satellite transmission, computer-based learning and interactive video, which will occur as the CPE market increases, allowing economies of scale to develop to make the technology more cost effective. These developments will assist in meeting the need for CPE packaged in innovative ways to permit greater participation by accountants with minimal disruption to work time and obligations.

Acknowledgements

The author gratefully acknowledges the information kindly provided by Mr Alan Blewett, Director of Education and Professional Development of the ICA, and Mr Michael Farkas, Director of Professional Development of the ASA.

References

Australian Society of Accountants. (1987). *Annual report, 1987*. Melbourne: ASA.
Australian Society of Accountants. (1985). *Annual report, 1985*. Melbourne: ASA.
Birkett, W. P. (1980). *Continuing education and the professional development of accountants*. Proceedings of the NSW State Congress, Australian Society of Accountants, March.
Buckley, J. W., & Weston, J. F. (1980). *Regulation and the accounting profession*. Wadsworth: California.
Carey, J L. (1969). *The rise of the accounting profession*. New York, NY: AICPA.
Cook, R. B. D. (1978). What members think about compulsory professional development. *The Australian Accountant*. October, 548–552.
Farrell, B. J. (1986). *Accounting in perspective*. Sydney: Study Panorama Publishing Co.
Graham, A. (1978). *Without fear or favour*. Sydney: ICA.
Institute of Chartered Accountants in Australia. (1985). *Annual report, 1985*. Sydney: ICA.
Institute of Chartered Accountants in Australia. (1985). *Charting a dynamic future . . . Report of the Future Directions Committee of The Institute of Chartered Accountants in Australia*. Sydney: ICA.
Institute of Chartered Accountants in Australia. (1987). *Annual report, 1987*. Sydney: ICA.
Institute of Chartered Accountants in Australia. (1987). *Members' Handbook*, p. 23070, para 3. (First issued 1985.) Sydney: ICA.
Kirby, M. D. Mr Justice. (1980). Reform of professions. *The Australian Accountant*, September, 516–525.
Matthews, M R. (1981). *Continuing education: The new defense of professionalism*. Discussion Paper No. 3. Palmerston Nth, New Zealand: Massey University, Department of Accounting and Finance.
McKeon, A. (1978). The society gears up short course programme. *The Australian Accountant*, November, 632–636.
McLean, D. R. (1974). Professional development: The myth and the reality. *The Australian Accountant*, August, 428–432.
Miller, J. O. (1979). Academic preparation and continuing education of accountants. *The Chartered Accountant in Australia*, December, 23–28.
Miller, J. O. (1984). *Training for a profession: The early years in accounting*. VCTA Publishing.

Newman, R. L. (1980). Accounting education in the eighties. *Accounting Forum*, September, 5–14.

Poole, L. (1987). PD courses — A rural dilemma: NSW and Queensland. *The Chartered Accountant in Australia*, August, 33–36.

Pryor, K. W. (1983). CPD Task Force report. *The Australian Accountant*, Jan.–Feb., 10–11.

Russell, J. S. (1972). Professional development: Can you afford to do without it?. *The Australian Accountant*, September, 343.

Russell, J. S. (1973). The trend towards compulsory professional development. *The Australian Accountant*, April, 166–169.

Russell, J. S. (1976). Compulsory professional development: Yes or no. *The Australian Accountant*, June, 275–279.

Winfield, R. R. (1980). The future of accounting education in Australia. *Accounting Forum*, 15–17.

Wright, B. (1986). A view of the future. *The Australian Accountant*, July, 12–13.

6
The Engineering Profession
CYRIL STREATFIELD

Contextual factors

The title 'engineer' has a number of different meanings; the *Concise Oxford Dictionary* lists six different groups of people who have some claim to it. The two groupings which best describe the Professional Engineer are:

1 One who works in a branch of engineering (chemical, electrical, mechanical, civil) especially as a qualified professional; and
2 A person with special skill in treatment of human problems (a human engineer).

The original engineers were used in armies to build (or destroy) fortifications and the term 'civil engineer' was coined to distinguish engineers working in civilian occupations from their military counterparts. In the 19th century some engineers began giving themselves titles such as 'mechanical engineer' or 'electrical engineer' and different societies were formed to cater for the interests of the specialist groups. These were the forerunners of the professional institutions of which the oldest is the Institution of Civil Engineers in the United Kingdom, founded in 1828.

In Australia the tendency for different kinds of engineers to form their own institutions has been largely resisted, with one or two exceptions, and the Institution of Engineers, Australia (IEAust) caters for all of the various interests. A fairly recent development within the Institution has seen the formation of a number of specialist colleges, such as the College of Chemical Engineers, so that the particular interests of the different disciplines within engineering may be more adequately represented and catered for. An even newer venture is the commencement of Societies which will enable cross-discipline groups, such as those interested in computing, to get together on matters of common interest.

Corbett (1973) relates the background to the founding of the IEAust in 1919 and the granting of a Royal Charter in 1938. An amended Charter received Royal assent in 1988. The operation of the Institution is governed by a set of Bye-Laws and the professional conduct of individual members is prescribed by a Code of Ethics.

Most institution members fall into one of four categories:

1. Student Member — student undertaking an approved course;
2. Graduate Member — graduate of an approved course but with less than three years of approved professional experience;
3. Member — graduate of an approved course and with at least three years of approved professional experience; and
4. Fellow — same as for Member but with at least five years employment in positions of major engineering responsibility.

Members and Fellows are classed as Corporate Members and are entitled to describe themselves as Chartered Engineers (CEng). Students and Graduates are Non-Corporate Members and are not entitled to the 'CEng' designation. The June 1988 membership in all grades exceeded 43,500 distributed among all states and territories and including a number of members currently resident overseas. Local affairs are administered by Divisions with their headquarters in state capitals plus Newcastle and Canberra. Each Division has several specialist branches, such as electrical or mechanical. The national headquarters of the Institutuion is in Canberra.

Since 1980 all courses in Australia recognised by the Institution as providing an adequate basis for a career in professional engineering have contained the equivalent of at least four years of academic study at degree level at a university or college of advanced education. The content and level of the course material and the available facilities are monitored by the Institution both initially and at regular intervals thereafter (about every five years). Applicants for membership with qualifications gained overseas are expected to have reached an equivalent standard to that of graduates from recognised courses in Australia.

The Royal Charter of the Institution defines a number of roles, many of which are appropriate to its learned society status. These include:

1 Ensuring that Institution members have an adequate knowledge of the theory and practice of engineering;
2 Providing for the delivery and holding of lectures, exhibitions, public meetings, classes and conferences calculated to advance education in engineering; and
3 Encouraging the study of engineering.

In addition to the obligations placed upon it by the Royal Charter, a number of determinations of the Australian Conciliation and Arbitration Commission, for example, the *Professional Engineers Award 1972* has defined a 'qualified engineer' as 'a person who is or is qualified to become a graduate member of the Institution of Engineers, Australia'. This definition lays upon the Institution the heavy responsibility of setting the standard of proficiency of the engineering profession in Australia. A related responsibility gives the Institution a key role in determining whether an applicant with an overseas engineering qualification should be approved for immigration. The Royal Charter obviously lays squarely upon the Institution the responsibility for maintaining the currency of its members' knowledge, or in other words, for providing them with continuing professional education.

Policy and objectives

The 'knowledge explosion' is a well-known feature of contemporary life but nowhere is the term more apposite than in engineering, where it exerts considerable pressure on undergraduate courses. Present university first-degree courses in engineering include much material that was unknown just a few years ago. No modern course which did not contain a substantial component of computing would be given any credence, and such is the pressure on time that additional subjects can only be inserted, or existing ones enhanced, if some other material is omitted. In the faster developing disciplines such as electrical or computer engineering, there is a constant pressure to insert new material at the expense of traditional. Despite all this, the rate of technological progress is such that within a very few years of completing a course engineering graduates find that much of their hard-won knowledge is obsolete. The term 'half-life' has been borrowed from nuclear physics and is used to represent the length of time which elapses from the date of graduation to the moment when half of the graduate's knowledge is obsolete. In engineering, depending upon the particular discipline, the half-life is estimated to be between three and six years. In this situation the necessity for CPE becomes obvious. Without it an engineer's stock of useful knowledge will steadily decrease while technology passes him or her by.

Today, pressure is also exerted on undergraduate course content from sources such as community perceptions of the need for engineers to protect the environment and the profession's wish for additional training in management principles. Again, one way out of the dilemma is to do no more than give a brief introduction to some topics during the undergraduate course and then treat them more fully in post-graduate training. However, the problem with this approach lies in ensuring that all those who need training in specific areas do, in fact, receive it. At present there is no general requirement in Australia for the licensing of engineers, although this may occur in the future.

Concern of the Profession with CPE

As mentioned above, many engineering practitioners have long been aware of the need to keep themselves up-to-date. In 1985 the IEAust appointed a National Working Party to examine, and make recommendations on, a policy on Continuing Education (CE) which might be adopted by the Council of the Institution. Some similar bodies overseas have a longer history of institutional involvement.

The National Working Party held a number of meetings and its members conferred widely with colleagues both within the profession and without. Studies were also undertaken of continuing education activities and policies adopted by other engineering bodies overseas and by other professions in Australia or elsewhere. A draft policy was then submitted to the Working Party's parent body, the Institution's Standing Committee on Engineering Education Policy, and thence to Council. After further discussion, and some amendment, Council adopted, in 1986, its official Policy on Continuing Education.

The defined objectives of the Institution's active involvement in the field of continuing education are listed in the policy document as:

1 Maintaining high standards of professional performance by all of its members throughout their careers;
2 Ensuring currency in engineering knowledge by its members;
3 Increasing individual engineering capability as a contribution to national development;
4 Providing a formal structure in support of personal continuing education activity for career development by its members;
5 Preserving and enhancing the professional standard of engineers; and
6 Strengthening the role of the Institution as the regulator of engineering standards in Australia.

Having defined the objectives of the Institution's involvement in continuing education, the policy document goes on to list some of the ways in which these are to be achieved. The Institution is to:

1 Promote the undertaking by its members of an adequate level of continuing education or to demonstrate in other ways a continuing level of professional development;
2 Accord formal recognition to such achievements;
3 Ensure that appropriate continuing education opportunities are provided;
4 Provide for the accreditation of continuing education; and
5 Promote the support of relevant continuing education by the employers of professional engineers as a part of the employees' normal duties.

The policy contains a statement of intent to establish a defined minimum commitment to ongoing professional skills development, through education. A recommended minimum is an average of 150 hours per triennium on a rolling basis. Details of acceptable types of continuing education are contained in the appendices to the policy statement (IEAust, 1986).

Recognised Forms of CPE

The IEAust policy document defines continuing education as 'the formal study undertaken by engineers to extend or update their knowledge or to fit them to meet advances or changes of direction in their careers'. The following list gives types of formal education which are recognised as complying with the definition:

1. Higher degree and graduate diploma studies;
2. Short courses conducted by:
   (a) educational establishments,
   (b) private firms,
   (c) government and semi-government departments,
   (d) professional institutions;
3. Individual undergraduate or post-graduate course units not taken for award purposes;
4. Workshops;
5. Seminars;
6. Symposia;
7. Conferences;
8. Technical meetings (e.g. Branch meetings); and
9. Forums.

The policy document goes on to state:

> Execution of the continuing education process may be by direct participation or by means of 'Distance Learning' techniques.
>
> Acceptable activities encompass those available for unrestricted application for enrolment and those conducted for restricted groups for proprietary reasons, provided that they meet the Institution's criteria for accreditation. (IEAust, 1986)

The policy statement does not limit continuing education activities to narrow technical fields. They may encompass not only 'all existing and emerging areas of the science and practice of engineering which engage members during their professional careers' but also fields such as project management, psychology/behavioural science, economics, computer applications, financial management, negotiation skills, labour relations, environmental issues, marketing, health and safety, communication skills, law (contract, industrial, commercial), management principles, budgetting and control, organisation development, quality assurance.

Voluntary or Mandatory CPE?

The present policy document draws attention to the Institution's Code of Ethics and points out the responsibility of members for ensuring that they remain up-to-date during their careers. It is stated that the Institution accepts CE as an important element of professional development and it is recommended that members undertake a minimum of 50 hours per annum of appropriate CPE activities, averaged over three-year periods on a rolling basis. A pilot survey undertaken in 1987 showed that a majority already meet the recommended level.

At the time of writing the Institution has no mandatory requirement for CE. This situation is under frequent discussion and some challenge, and it may well be that changes will occur although the author would not like to forecast likely timings. Some of the considerations are:

1. In late 1986 the Institution set up a special 'Task Force' to develop basic policy recommendations on the future of engineering education in Australia. The Task Force report, entitled *Engineering Education to the Year 2000*, was adopted by Council with some minor caveats and contains the recommendation that 'the continuing education policy of the Institution should be promoted and strengthened with all engineers required to pursue continuing education' (Task Force on Engineering Education, 1987, Recommendation 4–17);
2. In a reorganisation of Institution membership structures it will be possible for IEAust members to be members of a specialist College as well as being members of the Institution as a whole. One possible development is that a College may require evidence of satisfactory continuing education for admission to, or maintenance of, membership; and
3. When applying for transfer to a higher grade of membership of the Institution, for example from Graduate to Member or from Member to Fellow, it is likely that an applicant will be expected to demonstrate that he or she has complied with the Institution's Policy on Continuing Education.

Priority Groups for CPE

It is difficult to identify any particular group of engineers that is more in need of CPE than another. The aforementioned knowledge explosion recognises no boundaries and the mobility of the profession in terms of interests, activities, locations, responsibilities, etc. ensures a continual need for all members to refresh their capabilities. Many senior members are grappling with computer systems while their younger colleagues are savouring the delights of the principles of labour relations or financial management.

Management

Because there is as yet no mandatory requirement for members to participate in continuing education, management mechanisms are still in an early and, in many ways, exploratory stage. As was noted above, a pilot survey was carried out in 1987 to determine the current level of members' involvement in continuing education. It is intended that this should in future become a general survey and a record of returns established and maintained. Obviously future patterns will largely be determined after resolution of the voluntary vs. mandatory debate.

The Institution maintains a Board of Education and Training, chaired by a Vice-president. This Board has responsibility for implementing the Institution's Continuing Education policies and making recommendations on changes and developments. Management mechanisms for CE activities have yet to be established.

Continuing Education Centre

The Victorian Division of the IEAust has established in Melbourne a Centre for Continuing Education, which may possibly become a national centre or else may simply serve as a pilot for similar establishments in other states. At the moment it acts as a recording centre for CE activities which are relevant to engineers but it will also have an endorsing role and is planning also to act as a provider where a specific need has been identified.

Program content and delivery

It will have been noticed from the descriptions of membership categories that upward movement through the categories requires a member to have had appropriate professional experience. Such experience is also often necessary when seeking promotion or change in employment. In the United Kingdom, the Engineering Council has produced a proposal

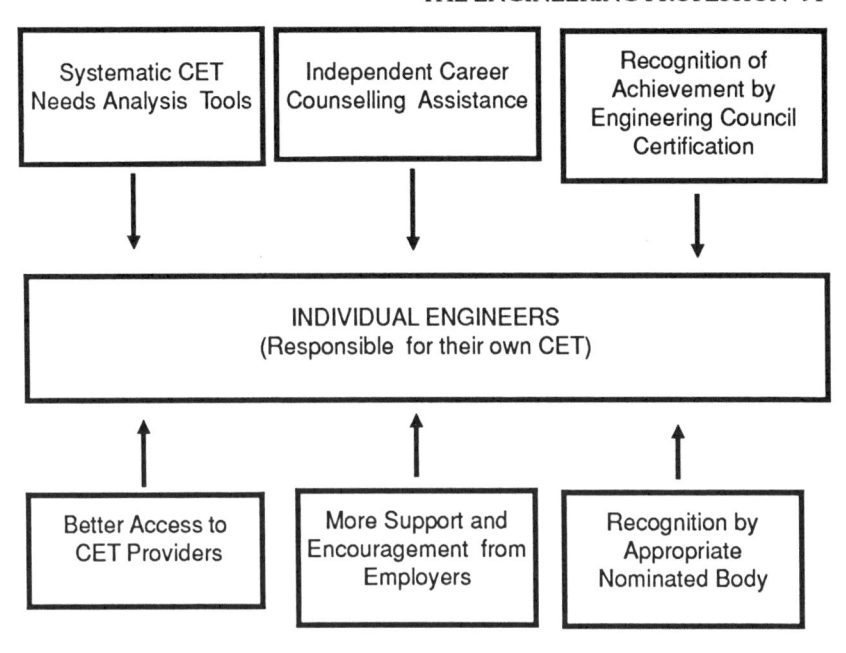

```
┌─────────────────┐  ┌─────────────────┐  ┌─────────────────┐
│  Systematic CET │  │Independent Career│  │  Recognition of │
│Needs Analysis Tools│ │Counselling Assistance│ │  Achievement by │
│                 │  │                 │  │Engineering Council│
│                 │  │                 │  │  Certification  │
└────────┬────────┘  └────────┬────────┘  └────────┬────────┘
         ↓                    ↓                    ↓
┌─────────────────────────────────────────────────────────┐
│                   INDIVIDUAL ENGINEERS                   │
│              (Responsible for their own CET)             │
└────────↑────────────────────↑────────────────────↑──────┘
┌─────────────────┐  ┌─────────────────┐  ┌─────────────────┐
│  Better Access to│  │ More Support and │  │  Recognition by │
│  CET Providers  │  │ Encouragement from│  │   Appropriate   │
│                 │  │    Employers    │  │  Nominated Body │
└─────────────────┘  └─────────────────┘  └─────────────────┘
```

Figure 6.1 The Main Elements of the National System for Engineers
Source: The Engineering Council Consultative Document.

for what it calls *a national system of Continuing Education and Training (CET) for engineers and technicians* (Engineering Council, 1988). Figure 6.1 (reproduced from the Engineering Council document, by permission) shows the main features of the proposal. It is an integrated scheme in which individuals are linked to Career Action Plan (CAP) advisers, and employers together with continuing education providers cooperate with the professional institutions and the Engineering Council to optimise the progression of a new graduate through the ranks of the profession. This interesting concept requires a great deal of organisation, and cooperation between the different parties if it is to be realised in any meaningful way.

In Australia planning is not yet as far advanced as that of the Engineering Council but there is increasing realisation of the importance of what is known as 'formation', that is, the process by which a raw university graduate becomes an experienced and capable engineer. The Institution is becoming more and more interested in the progression of a Graduate Member through to Corporate Member. This is a vital three-year (minimum) period in an engineer's career, too important to be left to chance or to the vagaries of opportunity, and the Institution hopes soon to be in a position to offer more worthwhile support and guidance.

Assessment of Need

Returning to the more specific topic of CE, the engineering profession has a wider range of interests than many others. The range is indeed enormous — from dams and bridges to aircraft and rockets; from off-shore oil exploration to semiconductors and integrated circuits; from electrical power systems to computers and robots; and almost anything else that can be named, not forgetting the management and financial aspects. It is thus not possible to find a simple CE program which will meet all requirements. There are, of course, some cross-disciplinary topics such as management, finance or protection of the environment which are of general interest but in other areas there has, in the past, been a tendency for CE programs to be *provider-driven*. This has often meant that courses have been offered because they are someone's special interest and in the hope that there will be sufficient enrolments to cover the costs. There is now a move towards a *demand-driven* situation where the potential customers are making their needs known and looking for appropriate people or organisations to meet them. Once again it must be said that mechanisms for assessing those needs are still in the formative stage, although some progress is being made.

Range of Topics Covered

The range of topics which may fairly be considered as CE for members of the engineering profession is almost limitless. Besides technical topics at any level between post-doctoral research and introductory courses in newly developing areas, engineers need to become involved in management, financial direction of organisations, economic planning, legal aspects, professional indemnity, labour relations and industrial safety. The list goes on and it is beyond the capability of any one organisation to meet the demand effectively.

Fortunately in Australia there is a large number of tertiary educational institutions which are able, and usually very willing, to provide appropriate courses in almost any topic at a wide range of levels. Under the provider-driven system it is not always certain that all needs are met but there is no doubt that where any specific need of sufficient magnitude is identified, someone will move to meet it. A current example of this may be found in post-graduate management studies. There is a general impression within the profession that top management positions in engineering organisations are more and more frequently being filled by non-engineers with management, or business qualifications such as the Master of Business Administration degree. There is thus a demand for suitable courses which will allow engineers to compete successfully for management appointments. Special courses that will enable engineers to gain post-graduate certificates or diplomas in management are now available.

At the present time the great majority of CPE activities are carried out in tertiary or similar institutions in the forms of lectures, seminars or workshops. Some course material is now available on audio- or video-cassettes and some correspondence courses are either in existence or in preparation. It is also known that at least one provider is actively examining the use of personal computers, either in computer-assisted learning packages or as terminals for interactive satellite communication programs. Many exciting developments of this sort are planned for the near future.

Cooperation amongst providers in program delivery of any kind is distinctly low key at present. This is not necessarily due to any antipathy or lack of desire but is often due to lack of information. One of the functions of a national recording centre, possibly modelled on the prototype in Victoria, would be to help eliminate unnecessary duplication, and also identify areas of inadequate coverage.

It is possible that courses are being provided in large government or industrial organisations for their own staff members which could be made available, with suitable financial arrangements, to outsiders. Any rationalisation or cooperation of this kind would benefit all parties concerned including the nation.

Evaluation

The Institution of Engineers, Australia has a comprehensive and well-structured procedure for the assessment of undergraduate courses leading to degrees in engineering. There are prescribed standards, and courses which satisfy these standards are given Institution recognition and are said to be 'accredited'. After considerable debate within the Institution it has been decided that, since a whole range of standards and levels is permissible within the IEAust Continuing Education Policy guidelines, the term 'accreditation' should not be used in that context.

However, there is a demonstrated need for some indication of the Institution's approval. Members who are considering enrolling in courses are asking whether they will be counted as approved CE whilst providers are wanting to use the Institution's name in their publicity material. Consideration is therefore being given to providing Institution 'endorsement' in appropriate cases. All the implications of this have not yet been fully explored but some possibilities are:

1 Block endorsement for courses provided by some tertiary educational institutions;
2 Endorsement for courses which are presented a number of times with little variation, on the basis of reports from participants; and
3 Provisional endorsement for 'one-off' courses on the basis of notes or other material, subject to confirmation after receipt of reports from participants.

Recording of Attendances

Two methods of recording members' participation in continuing education activities are likely to be installed: an annual census during which members will make a return of the hours they have devoted to continuing education during the previous three years; and a listing of participants by providers of 'endorsed' activities.

Finance

Continuing education comes in a number of forms, most of them costly in time or money, or both. The current thinking is that most CE activities should be self-funding. This principle applies equally to university courses, college of advanced education courses and courses provided by commercial organisations.

Governments can encourage participation in CE by reducing the financial cost to individuals, or by setting an example and making it easier for their own employees to attend courses or other CPE activities. Some kind of incentive could also be given to employers in this latter regard. On the other hand, if a government determines that a *user-pays* principle would be appropriate, then many individuals might find the costs of some types of continuing education to be more than they are prepared to pay. The Institution advocates a *beneficiary-pays* system, in which costs are shared among the various beneficiaries such as the participants, the employers and, in some cases, the community. That is, it must be acknowledged that the participant is often not the only beneficiary. Employers and the community at large sometimes also benefit from an increase in an engineer's knowledge or skills and should be prepared to contribute to the costs in some equitable way. A more efficient and highly qualified workforce is undeniably a community asset. In particular instances when the potential benefit accruing to the community is very high, such as is the case with higher degrees which train students in research methods, then the community should bear most, if not all, the costs.

Likely future developments

Most of the likely future developments have already been discussed in the text. It is expected that there will be an increase in availability of suitable CE activities; 'endorsement' of courses will become common; mandatory continuing education of some kind may be adopted by the Institution; a Career Advancement Plan (CAP) will become a feature of the early professional life of new engineering graduates; and undergraduate course material may be supplemented by CE so as to provide relief from the incessant pressure to include more topics.

There is no doubt that the engineering profession in Australia is fully aware of its responsibilities and of the implications of the knowledge explosion. Obsolescence of knowledge can only be counteracted by updating or extending such knowledge and the Institution is committed to continuing education as an essential component of the maintenance of the standards of the qualifications of its members.

References

Australian Conciliation and Arbitration Commission. (1972). *Professional Engineers (General Industries) Award 1972*, handed down by Commissioner Barnes. Sydney, 18 February.

Corbett, A. H. (1973). *The history of the Institution of Engineers, Australia.* Sydney: The Institution of Engineers, Australia, in association with Angus & Robertson Publishers.

Engineering Council (UK). (1988). *Continuing education and training — A national system for engineering.* A consultative document. January.

Institution of Engineers, Australia. (1986). *Policy on continuing education.* Canberra, 31 October.

Task Force on Engineering Education. (1987). *Engineering education to the year 2000.* A report to the Council of the Institution of Engineers, Australia. Canberra, October.

7
The Profession of Occupational Therapy
GWYNNYTH LLEWELLYN

Contextual factors

Occupational therapy, a relatively new health profession, was pioneered in Australia during the Second World War in response to the need to rehabilitate soldiers for return to service. Rehabilitation took place in military hospitals under the direction of medical practitioners, most of whom were male. The influence of the wartime situation on the early development of the profession is reflected both in the first educational courses known as 'War Emergency Courses', and in the gender of the participants, all female.

The task of soldier rehabilitation was obviously a task for women: who else was there? As Anderson and Bell (1988) note in their recent history of occupational therapy in Australia, the stereotype of the occupational therapist in a female role was apparent from the beginning of the profession. After the war women occupational therapists, along with women in other areas of employment, returned to their 'rightful' place—in the home—to raise a family and support the male bread-winner. Occupational therapy then came to be seen as a suitable occupation prior to marriage, particularly for young middle-class women.

The predominance of values generally associated with women in a subservient role continued throughout the 1960s. However, other values such as further learning and skill development beyond initial training gradually received recognition. Elizabeth Hudson in her presidential address to the 4th Federal Conference of the Australian Association of

Occupational Therapists in 1966, mentioned the desire for postgraduate knowledge and techniques as well as the following essential qualities for occupational therapists: enthusiasm and inspiration, dedication and the willingness to serve, tolerance, humility and understanding.

Within ten years personal attributes were relegated to second place as academic ability was required to meet the developing scientific base in occupational therapy education. In 1976 a three-year Bachelor of Applied Science Degree in Occupational Therapy was introduced in New South Wales, and in 1981 this was extended to a three-and-a-half year degree course (Queensland, ahead of the other states, had a combined degree course with Physiotherapy from 1950).

However, a degree course does not of itself determine a career-oriented view for members of a profession. The National Survey of the Occupational Therapy Labour Force (Australian Association of Occupational Therapists, 1981) noted that occupational therapy was a predominantly female profession of which approximately half of the members were under 30 years of age. Although three-quarters of the respondents were practising, only 63 per cent were practising full-time. Just over half of all respondents had participated in CPE activities over the preceding year although, as defined by the survey, this only included attendance at courses.

In 1981 only 25 per cent of occupational therapists planned to continue in the profession for ten years or more. The trend was for them to work full-time in the period after graduation, then to become involved in home duties after marriage, then return to practise on a part-time basis. A more recent study of New South Wales occupational therapy students by Nordholm and Westbrook investigated the change in attitudes towards self, career, and women's roles during the period 1976 to 1986. These authors found that:

> In 1986, incoming students had higher aspirations and greater career commitments. They were more likely to plan full-time careers combined with child-rearing.
>
> Work values such as respect received, friendliness of co-workers, doing something worthwhile, job security and promotion opportunities were seen as more important by the 1986 students. (Nordholm & Westbrook, 1987, p. 103)

Whether the attitude changes demonstrated by these students will be reflected in graduates remaining in the profession for longer and seeking more CPE and promotion opportunities remains to be seen. The following brief discussion of the organisational structure of the profession in Australia will help clarify the situation into which these new graduates will go.

Organisational Structure of the Profession

Occupational therapists work within a variety of health, education and welfare organisations in both government and non-government sectors. Therapists are also employed in industry, as consultants, or in private practice either independently or in conjunction with other disciplines. Professional organisation management structure is two-tiered. The first tier is the Australian Association of Occupational Therapists Incorporated which is made up of member organisations from the states and territories. Presently, the smallest association (Northern Territory) has 20 members and the largest (Victoria) approximately 700 with the total number of occupational therapists throughout Australia who are members of their association approaching 3000.

Individual occupational therapists join their state or territory association and part of the membership fee is allocated to the parent body for activities such as maintaining a national executive, production of a journal, granting awards and so on. Since the inception of this national association in 1956 CPE has been part of the stated objectives. In the constitution which was accepted on incorporation of the Association in 1985, one of the objects for which the Association is established is 'to conduct seminars, workshops, conferences or any other activities which promote the level of expertise within the profession of occupational therapy' (Australian Association of Occupational Therapists, 1985).

With two exceptions CPE activities are more usually within the province of the state or territory associations. The two exceptions are the endorsement of the Certification Course in the Administration and Interpretation of the Southern California Sensory Integration Tests and the organisation of a federal biennial conference.

Registration for occupational therapists is not federally required in Australia: at present only Queensland, Western Australia and South Australia have registration boards. To be employed in the other states and territories occupational therapists must be eligible for membership of their association. This requires proof of qualifications gained in a course in occupational therapy approved by the World Federation of

Occupational Therapists or of having satisfied the requirements of the Committee of Overseas Professional Qualifications Examination. None of the states where registration is in force requires evidence of participation in further education or clinical experience for renewal of registration.

The second tier of professional organisation is the state or territory association to which individual occupational therapists belong. This is the level at which the majority of continuing education opportunities are organised, sponsored, promoted or at the very least, facilitated in consultation with special interest or geographical groups. Each state or territory has a somewhat different structure. However there is come commonality in objectives, concerns and difficulties encountered.

The remainder of this chapter addresses Chapter 3 issues involved in providing CPE to this relatively small and predominantly female profession spread through a variety of agencies in both the government and private sectors. The themes common to occupational therapists throughout Australia will be illustrated by examples across the states. Issues more relevant in certain settings are included with specific examples as appropriate.

Policy and objectives

The primary objective of the state or territory associations is to enhance the profession of occupational therapy. Continuing professional education is seen to be an integral part of the promotion of the profession through the growth of knowledge and skills and the maintenance of standards. In principle, CPE has been on the agenda of the associations since their inception. In practice, the provision of CPE opportunities fluctuates with the time available and the enthusiasm of individuals or groups to undertake the organisation of these activities. This is particularly so in the smaller organisations where numbers are limited and many tasks have to be shared by a few. However, often the sense of isolation which may be strongly felt by a smaller or distant group gives an added impetus. In Tasmania, for example, despite a small membership of 58, at least one, and often several education sessions, is held each year.

At the association level the commitment to CPE is demonstrated by at least one executive member having this portfolio or being elected as

CPE convenor. This person may work with a committee (more usual in the larger states) or may coopt people to assist, as the occasion demands. All involvement in the executive, committee or through coopting is voluntary with members providing their time after work or on weekends. Although there is a certain amount of professional pressure applied to therapists to be involved in their professional association, there is little obvious reward for the effort.

In some states, for example Queensland and Victoria, the primary task of the executive member or convenor is to coordinate all CPE activities. Much of the organisation, planning and implementing of the activities is undertaken by a special interest group which identifies the need, seeks approval and in some cases funding from the association, and then proceeds to implement the activity. Special interest groups cover a range of specialty areas such as mental health, private practice, computers, gerontology and quality assurance.

The New South Wales Association of Occupational Therapists operates somewhat differently. In this state almost all CPE activities are totally managed through the special interest groups which are more able to respond directly to the particular needs of their members. The state body, on the other hand, organises courses which are likely to attract therapists from a range of areas of professional practice. This may also include organising workshops or seminars around the visits of international speakers.

Individual occupational therapists are well indoctrinated into being members of a profession. In New South Wales a commitment to professionalism is addressed at the undergraduate level through two aims of the curriculum: demonstration of personal characteristics consistent with the Australian Association of Occupational Therapists Code of Ethics and demonstration of responsibility for professional education and development (Cumberland College of Health Sciences, 1986). A study by Robertson (1986) suggests that this emphasis is reflected in the participation rates of New South Wales occupational therapists in CPE activities. Overall attendance in the preceding 12 months for her sample of 128 therapists ranged from 81 per cent for short courses, seminars and conferences to 25 per cent for postgraduate courses. In addition, a clear majority of the respondents (approximately 95 per cent) stated that they engaged in informal CPE activities such as reading professional literature.

These participation rates suggest that occupational therapists put a high value on professional development beyond their initial professional education. It is important to note here that none of the activities referred to above, with the exception of postgraduate courses, count for credit nor are there any mandatory CPE requirements for therapists remaining in, or returning to, the workforce. The issue of credit for courses undertaken has been discussed at length in all states. Currently Queensland is again examining the possibility of accruing credits from association courses and those conducted by other educational bodies. In those states and territories without registration, achieving some form of registration or certification tends to take precedence over credit or mandatory CPE issues.

Attendance at all CPE activities is voluntary, so it is assumed that what matters for the participants is personal learning. The fact that CPE for occupational therapists is voluntary has had a direct effect on the type of activities offered. The activities usually relate specifically to the workplace, either in the form of a new or alternative treatment method or technique for a particular client group, or as sessions which involve self exploration such as stress management or bereavement counselling to help therapists find new ways of dealing with particular workplace situations. In addition, some educational activities at a broader level may be presented, such as medico-legal aspects of care, implementation and maintenance of standards and research promotion. It would be rare, even in the larger states, to attract therapists to a workshop which focused entirely on theory, conceptual frameworks or principles of service delivery.

There has been a change in the provision of CPE activities for occupational therapists across Australia. Initially more emphasis was placed on learning through experience: in the 1970s and 1980s formal continuing education activities have become more usual. This change is also reflected in the development of state associations. When an association is small and in the early stages of development, specific treatment-oriented content is the primary focus. With the growth of the association, members develop special interest groups to address issues associated with their particular area of professional practice. The state association is then able to provide activities which cover a broader range of issues pertinent to all members, regardless of their speciality area. At the present time however, these state-wide activities still deal mainly with issues which relate to the day-to-day practice of the profession. It will be interesting to note whether the next stage of development leads to the provision of opportunities for therapists to share more 'theoretical' concerns.

Management

Throughout Australia the focus of CPE activities is determined by the associations' responding to requests from members. Usually individuals or small groups of members identify a particular need and subsequently work through their association structure to gain support, either organisational or financial, or in some cases both, to have this need met. Consequently, needs in the areas of professional practice with the largest numbers or the most vocal members are more frequently met. In some states, for example Tasmania, there is recognition at the association level that some areas of professional practice are grossly under-served. With few therapists working in these areas (which may differ from state to state) organisation of CPE activities to meet their specific needs is unlikely to occur in the near future.

There is a chronic shortage of practising occupational therapists in Australia. It would be reasonable, therefore, to assume that providing CPE activities for non-practising therapists would be a priority. In fact, little has been done in this area despite some promising beginnings. In 1986 a six-week refresher course was developed by Cumberland College of Health Sciences and supported by the Skills in Demand Program of the New South Wales Department of Employment and Industrial Relations. In the following two years, despite initial advertising for a repeat of this course, no further courses have been funded. In Victoria the association has tried to meet the needs of non-practising therapists using two different approaches: the first was a three-month tutorial and hands-on refresher program and the second, through individually organised intern-type programs in specific areas of professional interest.

Program content and delivery

Generally speaking, CPE activities for occupational therapists in Australia are not part of a structured program of CPE. Continuing professional education activities rarely have specific prerequisites such as attendance at a previous course or workshop. The content in most activities is designed to be relevant to both the inexperienced and experienced practitioner. This often results, not surprisingly, in disappointment for both groups as the level of information is perceived as either too general or, alternatively, too advanced. In some states this issue is currently being addressed through the provision of basic and advanced workshops; however, this attempt is still some way from the provision of a coordinated, sequenced learning program.

Several states in recent years have conducted surveys through their newsletters in an effort to respond more closely to their members' needs. The type of information gathered relates mainly to topics and content, length and timing of activities, and costs the member is prepared to pay. Issues such as level of information required, desired learning experiences, or alternative teaching methods that may be preferred are only occasionally addressed.

Continuing professional education activities are usually offered in the 'tried and true' formats of lecture and small group discussion, with notable exceptions in the areas of expressive arts (generally experiential) and in certain technical areas where practical experience is an essential part of the learning process. Lecture and or workshop sessions are mainly held in capital cities or large country centres: this creates travel and cost problems for therapists living in geographically remote areas. In Queensland the association has tried to help these therapists by providing sponsorship for one remote therapist per CPE activity if the therapist is without employer assistance. In an attempt to supply information to therapists unable to attend workshops, for whatever reason, some special interest groups have set up resource centres which contain not only relevant reading material for loan, but also tapes, often both audio and video, of CPE workshops.

Although many groups would like to see distance education methods used to provide information to remote therapists, this remains an ideal for the future given that the membership of each association is still relatively small, the executive and committee members are all voluntary, and the major source of funds is membership subscriptions.

In all states links have been established with other health professional groups, in particular, physiotherapists and speech pathologists, and it is not uncommon for activities to be offered jointly with members of these professions. In recent years this has spread further to include groups such as architects, occupational health and safety engineers, and horticulturists. Not all states have an institution that provides an education for the profession of occupational therapy. However, where one does exist there is usually some degree of cooperation between the association and the institution in the provision of CPE activities. This cooperation may range from the institution providing rooms or resources for workshops, or providing the services of the faculty as workshop leaders, to a course being conducted through the institution's Department of Continuing Education on behalf of the association.

Commercial involvement in the provision of CPE to occupational therapists has occurred in areas of practice where commercially available products, such as splinting materials, are part of the treatment program. In one case a commercial organisation runs regular workshops in conjunction with the association on a regular basis, at both a basic and advanced level and in a weekday and weekend format. Such cooperative efforts, whether with other professional groups, educational institutions or commercial enterprises, are at a relatively informal level and are somewhat under utilised.

Evaluation

Evaluation of CPE activities is not generally accorded a high priority. Some accountability is often required by the organisation supporting the activity, either the state association or the special interest group. This mostly relates to adequate financial management, and in particular, to ensuring that activities are self-supporting. Success or failure of the activity is usually monitored by the workshop organisers on a fairly subjective basis, taking into account demand for places, comments from participants and the views of the participating speakers. Usually a short evaluation form of about one page in length is given to the participants at the conclusion of the activity and the responses are then collated for future planning. These forms deal with issues such as level of presentation, usefulness of activity related to workplace application and ideas for future workshops in the same or a related area.

Finance

Continuing professional education activities are seen to be one function of the associations which should be self-supporting. In New South Wales, for example, the special interest groups are expected to organise and manage their activities without financial support from the state association. However, in both Queensland and Victoria an amount is provided from the association to each special interest group as seeding funds: beyond this amount the activities are expected to cover costs. Consequently, for all activities a charge is made. Although there has been conjecture about whether a charge deters some possible participants such as new graduates or non-practising therapists, there is no reliable evidence to support this.

In the past occupational therapists working for private organisations have had some difficulties in participating in CPE due to a lack of recognition of its importance by their employer. Therapists wishing to attend had to do so in their own time and at their own expense. At times, and in certain situations, therapists working in the public sector have been similarly affected. As policy and resource allocation varies throughout Australia, it is not possible to generalise on this point. Suffice it to say, that in some employment situations financial and time support for CPE is seen to be in the employers' domain; in other instances, the individual is expected to use their own time and to attend at their own expense. It would be reasonable to assume that support, or lack of it, would affect participation rates. Unfortunately, no data are available on this, although a subjective impression suggests that in recent years, and in some states, more weekday activities have been scheduled and are fully subscribed.

Likely future developments

Continuing professional education for occupational therapists in Australia has developed in the last decade from informal sharing and collegial discussions to a relatively organised system of regular activities provided at the state level through special interest groups in the various areas of professional practice. Additionally, some activities are conducted through the educational institutions or in cooperation with other professional groups and a small number of commercial organisations. Biennial state conferences have now been established in several states; these offer more local input and thus complement the biennial federal conference which moves from state to state.

A range of opportunities exists for the occupational therapist who is seeking organised CPE activities. The extent of this range however, is dependent on the therapists' geographical location, place of work and particular area of professional practice. Non-organised activities such as reading professional literature and engaging in discussions with other professionals can occur of course, regardless of these restraints. Participation remains at a purely voluntary level, and despite peer pressure to be involved in CPE there are no legal or employment requirements to participate, either for those therapists in the workforce or for those therapists planning to re-enter the workforce after some years absence.

To return briefly to participation rates using New South Wales figures as an example. The figure for practising New South Wales occupational therapists in the 1981 national survey was 56.6 per cent (Australian Association of Occupational Therapists, 1981). This figure relates only to courses and does not include any other form of CPE. Robertson's survey of New South Wales occupational therapists conducted in 1984 showed that 81.1 per cent attended courses whilst 94.6 per cent engaged in professionally related reading activity (Robertson, 1984). An interesting finding showed that this group of occupational therapists was very keen to participate in CPE (100 per cent of respondents being in favour of CPE) and that preference for this reflects an almost equal split between those who prefer to participate on a more formal level and those who prefer more informal participation. It would seem that although there is no mandatory requirement, many occupational therapists in fact regard CPE as 'compulsory' if they wish to be involved in the profession as up-to-date, competent and effective practitioners.

As noted elsewhere (Maple, 1987) several issues need to be addressed in relation to the provision of CPE for occupational therapists in New South Wales. I would like to suggest here that these issues have the same relevance for occupational therapists throughout Australia. Issues for the profession include provision of formal and/or informal CPE activities, credit systems for approved courses, distance leaning, and measurement of the application of knowledge and skills learnt to the workplace. For the individual the relevance of these CPE activities to professional practice, the availability and accessibility of suitable activities, the appropriateness of the instruction to the participants' time, resources and learning style, and the credibility of the activities in the eyes of the profession and possibly the employing body are paramount.

The challenge for occupational therapy in the 1990s will be to address and resolve these issues within the following parameters: a predominantly female profession, with a high attrition due to home duties or part-time employment, and with an organisational structure which relies on commitment of time and energy from a few individuals over and above the demands of their professional employment. Despite the apparent size of the task, the gains made in the last ten years seem to suggest that this relatively new profession has made a healthy start in the provision of CPE activities for its members.

References

Anderson, B., & Bell, J. (1988). *Occupational therapy: Its place in Australia's history.* Sydney: NSW Association of Occupational Therapists.

Australian Association of Occupational Therapists. (1981). *National survey of the occupational therapy labour force.* Sydney: Author.

Australian Association of Occupational Therapists. (1985). *Constitution: Australian Association of Occupational Therapists.* Perth: Author.

Cumberland College of Health Sciences. (1986). *Bachelor of Applied Science (Occupational therapy): Stage 4 review.* Sydney: Author.

Maple, G. (1987). Continuing education for the health sciences: The voluntary/mandatory debate. *Australian Journal of Adult Education,* 27, 22–28.

Nordholm, L., & Westbrook, M. (1987). Changes in attitudes towards self, career, and women's roles among occupational therapy students. *Australian Occupational Therapy Journal,* 34, 89–104.

Robertson, S. (1986). Continuing education activities of occupational therapists in New South Wales. *Australian Occupational Therapy Journal,* 33, 47–54.

8
The School Teaching Profession
GLYN FRANCE

School teachers are Australia's largest professional group. In full-time equivalent terms there were 198,516 in 1987, an increase over the previous year of 0.4 per cent in government and 2.4 per cent in non-government schools, with 75 per cent of the profession employed in the former (Australian Bureau of Statistics, 1988). Teachers work with some three million students in widely differing school communities across six states and two territories. Both the size and diversity of the profession result in complex CPE needs and provisions, making generalisations across its sub-groups almost reckless. The very term 'continuing professional education' is more familiar in some settings than others and is used interchangeably in this chapter with 'inservice education' and 'professional development'.

As noted in Chapter 2, demographic data have important implications for CPE. For example, because almost two-thirds of teachers are women, many with their own children, the timing of CPE activities is important. Again, the changing age profile of the profession is relevant, and Table 8.1 (page 110), though providing data only for government school teachers in Victoria, reflects a 'middle-ageing' of the profession generally. New entrants to the profession have declined to some 5 per cent of all teachers annually, with the many young, newly graduated entrants of the 1970s now in or reaching mid-career, already on optimum salary in many instances and with limited career options.

Meanwhile, increasing cultural diversity in Australia, economic and technological changes, and higher expectations of schools add

Table 8.1 Median Age (years) of Classified Government School Teachers, Victoria, 1976 and 1985

Teacher category	1976	1985
Primary		
Male	32.9	37.2
Female	27.0	32.0
Total	28.4	33.0
Secondary (excluding Technical)		
Male	29.4	34.2
Female	26.5	31.7
Total	28.0	33.2
Technical		
Male	37.6	39.3
Female	30.3	33.4
Total	36.6	38.0

Source: *Compendiums of Statistics, 1976 and 1985*, Department of Education, Victoria.

dramatically to teacher needs in knowledge, skill, attitude and values appraisal, and often the reconceptualisation of the teaching role itself. Teaching continues to be a human service occupation requiring a high level of interpersonal skill and commitment. It follows that a variety of objectives within Scanlan's analysis (see Chapter 2) must be met by ongoing teacher education if it is to contribute to quality education in schools and better life chances for young people. Before examining current policy and program responses to this situation, some comment on the growth of teacher professionality in recent decades is necessary.

Teachers and the growth of professionality

In considering CPE for teachers, it is important to distinguish between 'professionalisation', with its industrial and status associations, and the growth of 'professionality', defined as 'the attitudes towards professional practice among members of an occupation and the degree of knowledge and skill which they bring to it' (Hoyle, 1980, p. 44). It is the enhancement of these attributes which is the goal of CPE.

On-the-job experience was, and probably still is, the dominant influence on levels of teacher professionality, though inservice education in various forms has for more than a century complemented it. The 1894 Conference and 1901 Summer School in Victoria, like the demonstration lessons, teacher exchanges, inspectorial systems and so on, were the responsibility of the state employing authorities. Preservice training left much to be desired: it is salutary to recall that in Victoria apprenticeship plus one year's pedagogical study was the preservice experience of primary teachers until 1951, whilst only after 1977 were universities involved in their training. However, as preservice education improved after 1945, practising teachers gained rather more autonomy in matters of professional development as subject and other associations brought them together, facilitating the informal learning from peers which is important in increasing proficiency.

Among the professional associations, two with national memberships over-riding state, sector and other divisions are illustrative of this trend. An important goal of the Australian College of Education, founded in 1959, is 'to create a fellowship of teachers, which will foster educational thought and practice and set before itself and the community the ethics of high professional responsibility' (Australian College of Education, 1960, p. 56). It provides a forum for professional development through conferences, working groups, publications (including *Unicorn*) and so on at local, chapter and national levels. The Australian Council for Educational Administration also conducts professional development programs at these levels, but adds an international perspective through the (British) Commonwealth Council for Educational Administration. However, though these two associations exhibit many of the conceptual, performance and collective identity features which Houle (see Chapter 1) associates with a dynamic profession, they directly involve no more than 3 or 4 per cent of teachers at the present time. Moreover, Bassett (1980) found that a smaller proportion of teachers belonged to professional organisations, including unions, in 1979 (71 per cent) than in 1963 (79 per cent), suggesting caution about the relative importance of the contribution of such associations to the growth of teacher professionality.

In traditional thought one distinguishing feature of a profession has been its basis in a body of knowledge and skill continually modified and improved by research. Local studies have added to professional self-knowledge (for example, Batten 1979; Bassett, 1980; Hughes, 1987). The Australian Council for Educational Research, founded in 1930, has in recent decades made a fundamental contribution to the profession through the dissemination of research results, publications such as the *Australian Journal of Education*, research monographs, the training of researchers, etc. For several years, until 1987, the Curriculum Development Centre in Canberra was a catalyst in educational thought. Whilst there is little doubt that Australian research and literature, like tertiary institutions as providers of inservice education, enhance teacher professionality, insufficient systematic data exist to assess their comparative impact on teaching practice. The 1970s in any event witnessed an unprecedented reliance on the inservice short course as a means of improving teaching.

The Commonwealth's Professional Development Program

The 1973 Report of the Interim Committee of the Schools Commission, (generally known as the Karmel Report) initiated a major national commitment to the resourcing of CPE for teachers in all school systems in Australia. Under what was known in its later stages as the Professional Development Program (PDP) $33 million was being made available annually by 1976 to state Development Committees, though this declined in real terms by two-thirds over the next ten years.

Initially the unprecedented generosity of government was in some ways counter-productive. The teaching profession was not ready for CPE on this scale and negative perceptions of inservice education persisted among some, whilst Commonwealth–State tensions were not entirely absent. The states had been providing courses to upgrade teacher qualifications and introduce new curricula, Tasmania had set up Teachers' Centres, and South Australia had developed a model of inservice delivery, including a residential training facility. But from 1974 a large increase in short courses and other opportunities such as one-year library courses and study grants became available to teachers, many of whom to that time had neither involvement in CPE nor saw its need. A compelling argument for greater investment in teacher development was, as in other countries, recognised by the Commonwealth Government, and subsequently its involvement and promotion of national objectives were largely to shape the further learning opportunities of teachers.

Three features of the PDP are relevant to an understanding of teacher professionality in the 1980s, even though states responded somewhat differently to the Program and one cannot yet assess its long-term impacts nationally. First, the Commonwealth took the position that inservice development should jointly involve government and non-government school systems in its administration and implementation. Thus in Victoria, for example, widely representative inter-system committees at state and regional levels formulated policies and allocated funds to government, Catholic and Independent schools. Not only did all sectors have greater access to tax-funded staff training, but practitioners from different backgrounds learnt from one another in specific areas (for example, computer use) and often put common professional interests ahead of politically divisive issues. It should be added that current Commonwealth policy is to direct funds to single school systems, as described later.

Another feature of the PDP was to devolve more responsibility for inservice education to regions and schools, consistent with other trends towards more localised decision making. Whilst it was a radical step for some schools, let alone teachers, to initiate submissions to inter-system committees implementing the Commonwealth Program, and for all sectors to have access to common teachers' centres, the reality of teacher empowerment in this respect rarely matched the rhetoric. For various reasons most initiatives came from employing authorities or their agencies, though subject and other professional associations profited from the new opportunities. Recognition of shared responsibility for their own development as a profession, and of the school and collegial group as important foci in staff training, nevertheless received some reinforcement.

In Chapter 2 it was noted that the relationship between the professional and the client is changing as the latter becomes more knowledgeable. An analogous process affecting teachers and parents was substantially supported by the PDP which, from 1977, funded parent involvement. In Victoria, where parents and older students participate alongside principals and teachers in educational policy making on school councils and regional boards, and where the professionals are technically responsible to school councils for implementing policy, inservice workshops and other activities are conducted often by parent organisations to disseminate information and develop skills in school governance. Teams of teachers, parents and students might work on curriculum. Members of the Australian Council of State School Organisations recently argued:

> The generalised knowledge of parents, teachers and students as well as the knowledge of other education professionals provide distinctive and complementary frameworks from within which to understand and contribute to education theory, policy and programs. (Brown, Cahir, & Reeve, 1987, p. 195)

If this premise about authority in teaching and learning is accepted, teachers need to be very clear about their professional mission.

The need for CPE for teachers

Teacher registration requirements are determined by the states and territories. In Victoria, for example, where three authorities administer regulations for the registration respectively of government primary, government post-primary and non-government teachers, permanent appointment to the teaching service of the Education Ministry can be gained in a number of ways, including possession of an approved Certificate of Proficiency in a trade, not less than eight years' experience in that trade, and an approved course of teacher training. Generally, teacher registration requires a minimum approved tertiary education and training of three years for primary teachers and four years for secondary teachers, or equivalent qualifications. Again there is much variation across states and territories, but Table 8.2 shows that these were the modal periods of preservice training for primary and secondary teachers in most government systems in 1979.

Initial training clearly cannot meet career-long needs. It is recognised — for example, by the Quality of Education Review Committee (1985) — that inservice education is essential to enable teachers to respond effectively to change in many areas, including the social, economic and cultural environment, curriculum content and organisation, pedagogy, student assessment, system and school organisation, and policy-making processes. New forms of technology impact on teaching methodology but also on student and social values generally. Changing educational

Table 8.2 Percentage Distribution of Government School Teachers by Years of Preservice Course, Australia, 1979

State or territory	Primary					Secondary				
	One or less	Two	Three	Four	Five or more	One or less	Two	Three	Four	Five or more
ACT	2	47	26	20	3	7	13	13	47	17
NSW	2	44	38	8	1	4	17	19	46	11
Vic.	6	25	54	6	2	11	12	5	54	14
QLD	13	31	50	3	–	15	23	26	29	5
SA	6	27	50	14	1	3	3	27	54	10
WA	2	32	57	3	1	4	16	37	33	7
Tas.	6	28	33	25	1	4	9	17	50	15

Source: *Teachers in Australian Schools*, 1979 (G. W. Bassett, 1980), pp. 121, 149, 177 and 205.

priorities make it increasingly necessary to reconceptualise the teaching role itself.

Meanwhile, high expectations of teachers in terms of their personal development continue:

> The teacher as a person needs to have developed a range of personal attributes: to be a well-educated person, to have integrated the knowledge derived from his studies and life experience ... to have developed mastery of at least one domain of knowledge ... to value excellence and scholarship ... to have a wide understanding of society ... to value all students whatever their cultural membership ... to be flexible ... to know himself, to reach an explicit understanding of the values which guide behaviour and aspirations. (National Inquiry into Teacher Education, 1980, pp. 51–52)

The traditional responsibility towards students is equally demanding: to develop in all students rational thinking ability, imagination, love of learning, judgement, creative self-expression, self-esteem, concern for others, skills for adult life and work, understanding of themselves and their world, as well as the foundation skills and employability. This responsibility necessitates on-going learning by teachers, the more so because they have to discharge it whilst responding to new expectations which exceed the role for which they were trained: to work in new relationships with parents; to understand labour-market influences on students and promote skills formation as part of national economic policy; to meet social justice goals in areas such as anti-discrimination, multicultural and Aboriginal education, and the integration of children with disabilities; to assume more policy-making responsibilities in devolved school systems; to develop curriculum, courses and classroom practices for a wider range of post-compulsory level students; and to assume major teaching and pastoral commitments to meet community needs, as, for example, in developing health education courses of the type described later in this chapter.

The changing age profile of the profession has been noted. Accompanying the increasingly middle-aged and mid-career predominance in a stalled career structure is a likely aversion to risk taking. Though teachers generally are both competent and well experienced, society is now demanding a higher level of skill in managing change. Those with experience reflect on aborted policy changes and classroom innovations, perceive often critical and uncomprehending community attitudes, and see little evidence in public debate of consensus even about the role of schools in society. Teacher attitudes, whether positive, negative or ambivalent, influence student learning. Perhaps for this reason it is more critical in teaching than some other professions that continuing education should explicitly aim at attitudinal as well as knowledge and skill development. Only if confidence, enthusiasm and renewal in the classroom role are enhanced will some teachers develop — and be able to communicate — attitudes and skills necessary to problem-solving in times of change. This in turn depends considerably on improved leadership skills among principals and middle managers, but above all on greater expertise in staff training in schools. If education is to contribute more directly to national goals, both generic and specific skill formation is essential for teachers in all sectors of the profession.

Policy responses to need

In view of the need it is perhaps surprising that participation in inservice education is not mandatory for continuing registration as a teacher or even for leadership roles. Several explanations are possible. First is the tenet that 'the truly professional person is self-motivating and accepts responsibility for seeking his/her own development' (Neal, 1987,

p. 352). A second explanation is more speculative, namely that mandatory requirements to update knowledge or skill may be linked with teacher evaluation, about which negative perceptions are common. A third explanation for the reliance on voluntary participation is the immense resource implications for governments and employing bodies in mandated inservice education. Even if tertiary resources were more fully used, the infrastructure for program delivery does not exist. It should be added that incentives in career advancement and remuneration are not a significant factor, though some tertiary institutions offer credit for substantial inservice education.

Policies at several levels govern the provision of continuing teacher education today and, because of the complexity involved, a much simplified review of the position in one state only will be attempted. Whilst Commonwealth policies imply some uniformity of objectives, structures, resources and accountability across Australia, there is scope for operational diversity among states and territories and non-government systems. School-level policies and practices also impact on opportunities open to teachers as, most obviously, when a particular school rules out inservice education in school time because of its disruption to teaching programs. Allowance must therefore be made for significant variations from the Victorian illustration which follows.

Under the PDP (which concluded in 1986) the Commonwealth had made efforts to direct its sharply declining resources to national goals in education, including teacher development activities in support of disadvantaged and isolated students and of Aborigines, girls, and parent participation in schools. In 1984 the Commonwealth also redirected funds from the Program to Special Purpose areas such as Participation and Equity, which was related to student retention to Year 12, Computer Education and, later, Basic Learning in Primary Schools. Each of these had its own funding components for teacher development. Rapid shifts of policy, lack of coordination and difficulties with accountability were structural factors limiting outcomes. It was found, for example, that of the total Commonwealth funds allocated to the English as a Second Language Program in 1984, investment in training or retraining was less than 0.5 per cent of program costs, since most went into payment by the Commonwealth of the salaries of teachers involved (Ingvarson & Coulter, 1987).

At present the Commonwealth negotiates with states and territories and with non-government authorities Resource Agreements which specify agreed national and system objectives and stringent accountability provisions. In Victoria, for example, Commonwealth funds of approximately $3.4 million were available in 1988 to the government system to meet some of the teacher development costs in areas considered of high priority by both levels of government. Funds are to be used to meet these priorities in approximately the proportions shown: general professional and staff development with a major emphasis on leadership and management skills of principals (56 per cent); teaching and assessment relating to the introduction of the Victorian Certificate of Education (14 per cent); implementation of Curriculum Framework guidelines (14 per cent); organisational improvement in schools (11 per cent); and staff development to assist the integration of children with disabilities into regular schools (5 per cent).

Again in Victoria, the state government system directs its own funds of some $0.5 million to defined priority areas: professional development to support the restructure of the school system; programs such as career education training and International Teaching Fellowships; and the development of consultancy skills in supporting the introduction of the Victorian Certificate of Education and some reimbursement of travel costs.

Of the Resource Agreement funds approximately one-third are applied to programs implementing policy priorities on a state-wide basis, and the balance applied through regional structures. At the regional level in Victoria 60 per cent of funds is allocated to a submission-based program which enables single schools or clusters to conduct inservice activities consistent with Resource Agreement priorities, and the remaining 40 per cent is applied through regional initiatives, for example in leadership training.

Thus, CPE opportunities for the majority of teachers are largely determined by policy frameworks set in place by governments. Teachers and schools acting locally have some scope within these frameworks to initiate programs by submission to their School Support Centres. It remains to be seen whether the new structures will provide the necessary degree of system coordination whilst allowing enough flexibility to schools to implement staff training policies to meet the personal and professional needs of specific groups and individuals on whom improved teaching and learning depend.

Program responses to need

Programs in CPE vary greatly in cost, content, duration and design. Two recent case studies will illustrate this. They will not convey the inherent inadequacies of the familiar annual inservice day attended perhaps by 100 teachers who, at a cost of less than $10 each, receive and discuss information on chosen topics as diverse as Literature in the Infant School, Bicycle Education, and Evaluation and Self-Concept, then to return to schools where there is little support for implementing change.

Nor will they convey the crusading social justice concerns of hundreds of teachers, parents and students who join an affirmative action network to remove sexist bias from school policies, textbooks and teaching and to conduct workshops on Mothers and Daughters in Computers, Work Experience for Girls, or Family Mathematics.

The cases, however, illustrate two broad avenues of continuing professional learning: one originating within a school with the efforts of practising teachers to develop new curriculum in response to student, parent and community concerns, the other originating outside the workplace when inservice educators and consultants work with classroom teachers to adapt and implement a strategy to improve teaching and learning. They suggest two distinctive, but not unrelated, approaches to inservice education: one in association with school-level development, the other with the dissemination of exemplary practice. They highlight one of the methodological issues underlying program responses to teacher needs.

Case Study 1

Staff at Westall Primary School, in an industrial part of Melbourne, improved their skills, acquired up-to-date knowledge, and deepened their cultural insights when, as a result of their concern for students and local media reports of drug abuse, teenage pregnancy and anti-social behaviour, they began work in 1986 on a Multicultural Health Education program. Existing curriculum guidelines were inadequate to meet the personal and community needs of this particular group of more than 400 children, 89 per cent of whom were from various ethnic backgrounds speaking 39 different languages. School-level curriculum development became a vehicle for teacher development over a period of two or three years.

In the sensitive, value-laden area of health education, interpersonal skills of a high order were necessary to gain the confidence of parents, many of whom were from cultural backgrounds as diverse as those of South America and Turkey, Laos and Mauritius. Teachers worked cooperatively with health professionals and interpreters in identifying what should — and could — be taught in this context about physical, mental and social health. They participated in a dozen inservice courses on Heart Health, Protective Behaviours, AIDS and so on, applying their learning to the curriculum. Perhaps most significantly they involved opinion leaders among the parent groups so that parents came to 'own' the curriculum, providing children with the security of shared understanding between home and school. At the same time teachers enhanced their own communication and leadership skills in extending their role into the community as professional educators. As in other occupations, experiential, on-the-job learning is an important component of continuing education if it is effectively exploited. For this, school-based personnel with expertise in staff development are necessary.

It is almost impossible to calculate teacher education costs in the Westall situation. Teachers gave personal time generously, and the school had to assemble resources from various Commonwealth and state agencies.

Case Study 2

The second case, Key Group, was however funded under the Commonwealth program Basic Learning in Primary Schools. The estimated cost was $1400 per teacher, compared with a per capita annual investment in professional development of government teachers of $347 in Victoria and $386 across Australia in 1984 (Ingvarson & Coulter, 1987). Key Group illustrates the dissemination of successful development processes which build teacher confidence in change management and problem solving in areas of curriculum and administration.

Teachers choose to join a Key Group, which in this case comprised three teachers, three parents and a local consultant. The focus was improved teaching and learning in mathematics. The Group identified its objective, attended a residential workshop with other Groups, developed and implemented an action plan, and further explored the learning experience with peers. In the workshop leaders modelled mathematics teaching and introduced participants to skills and theoretical insights in both teaching and action research. In their schools teachers worked with colleagues and parents to apply learning to classroom practice. Responsibility for improvement remained with the practitioner, and the capacity to reflect critically on practice and interrelate theory and practice was enhanced over the several months of the program.

Many approaches are taken to professional development in schools, but the most effective exhibit these design features:

- Clear perception of program goals and adult learning processes.
- Strategies to strengthen individual and group commitment to work-related problem solving and change management.
- The presentation of theory and use of demonstration, feedback, coaching, networking and other techniques appropriate to learning objectives.
- Enhancement of experiential learning skills of action, reflection, conceptualisation and experimentation.
- Provision for follow-through activities and development of insight and skill over time.
- Strategies to graft new learning into the school culture through school community collaboration within a coherent policy framework.

Among examples of successful programs are the Early Literacy Inservice Course developed in South Australia in the light of New Zealand and American experience, Tasmania's Centre for Continuing Education courses, and the Mathematics Inservice Course in the Australian Capital Territory.

Some issues in CPE for teachers

The professional issue for the teacher may be: How do I receive practical help in extending computer use in my classes? or, How do I cope with the seemingly ever-widening range of student abilities, interests and motivations? For the principal it may be: How do I exercise educational leadership collaboratively in a complex school community whilst being an effective line manager in a corporate management structure? These questions suggest the professional growth points in the workplace, and behind them — often determining the answers — are larger questions.

Given the politicisation of education, including inservice development, and policy making often dictated by economic expediency, what should be the role of the Commonwealth in continuing professional education? Are there essentially national goals in this field, and if there are, how should the central government ensure a successful focus on these through states and territories, government and non-government systems, schools, and professional associations?

Will Commonwealth–States Resource Agreements provide a more stable environment in which systems can coordinate resources in an integrated approach to teacher, curriculum and school development? Can this be done with the commitment of teachers on whom improved teaching and learning depend, and also with the accommodation of personal–professional needs in managing change? How should accountability procedures be made to serve governments and employing authorities and simultaneously the purposes of professional improvement?

What, indeed, should be the stance of the teaching profession at this formative time? Should it, possibly through professional associations, including the Australian College of Education, position itself to influence policy-making processes much more directly than in the past? Should it take initiatives, for example, in pressing for mandatory inservice education, but on its own terms? Meanwhile, can the teaching profession unite nationally in a commitment to its own continuing education, and in doing so discharge its unique responsibility as a profession: to offer young people and the whole community a model of teaching and learning at its best?

References

Australian Bureau of Statistics. (1988). *National schools statistics collection, Australia, 1987*. Canberra: Author.
Australian College of Education. (1960). *Founders convention*. Melbourne: Author.
Bassett, G. W. (1980). *Teachers in Australian schools, 1979*. Melbourne: Australian College of Education.
Batten, M. (1979). *Report of a national evaluation of the Development Program*. Canberra: Commonwealth Schools Commission.
Brown, J., Cahir, P., & Reeve, P. (1987). The educational rationale for parent participation. *Unicorn*, 13, 195–201.

Hoyle, E. (1980). Professionalization and deprofessionalization in education. In E. Hoyle & J. Megarry (eds), *World yearbook of education 1980: Professional development of teachers* (pp. 42–54). London: Kogan Page.

Hughes, P. (ed.). *Better teachers for better schools.* Melbourne: Australian College of Education.

Ingvarson, L., & Coulter, F. (1987). Policies for professional development: The 1984 national review of teacher education. In P. Hughes (ed.), *Better teachers for better schools* (pp. 298–323). Melbourne: Australian College of Education.

Interim Committee of the Schools Commission. (Chairman: P. H. Karmel). (1973). *Schools in Australia.* Report. Canberra: Australian Government Publishing Service. ('The Karmel Report, 1973'.)

Karmel Report. *See* Interim Committee of the Schools Commission, 1973.

National Inquiry into Teacher Education. (Chairman: J. J. Auchmuty).(1980). *Report of the National Inquiry into Teacher Education.* Canberra: Australian Government Publishing Service.

Neal, W. D. (1987). Summary and implications. In P. Hughes (ed.), *Better teachers for better schools* (pp. 352–360). Melbourne: Australian College of Education.

Quality of Education Review Committee. (Chairman: P. H. Karmel). (1985). *Quality of education in Australia.* Canberra: Australian Government Publishing Service.

Western Australia. Committee of Inquiry into Teacher Education. (Chairman: R. L. Vickery). (1980). *Teacher education in Western Australia.* Perth: Government Printer.

Part Three
CONCLUSION

9
Summary and Emerging Issues
BARRIE BRENNAN

The professions described in the profiles cover a wide range of Australian professional life. The largest profession, teaching — with over 200,000 practitioners; accountants, numbering 70,000; and occupational therapy — with just 3000 members nationally — are included. The engineering profession is dominated by men; women are 62 per cent of the teaching service; occupational therapy has always been a predominantly female profession. While the legal profession can trace its origins in Australia to the establishment of the Supreme Court in New South Wales in 1824, occupational therapy emerged as a profession only 40 or so years ago, as a result of the Second World War.

The profiles illustrate some of the features detailed in Chapter 2. The teaching profession is ageing and there is an annual decline in new entrants to a level of 5 per cent of all teachers. Only 18 per cent of New South Wales solicitors are women but the entrants to study of the profession reflect more closely parity of the sexes. The engineering profile noted how the ASCO classification group, managers and administrators, was having an impact on their profession. Engineers wanted to gain managerial positions in competition with accountants. The occupational therapy and engineering professions have tried to cater for specialised interests in their membership by creating special colleges in the latter and special interest groups in the former.

The professional association was accorded significance in Chapter 2. In New South Wales, the Law Society has the power to license solicitors and to cancel their licences. The Institution of Engineers was established by Royal Charter. The profile on accountants noted two associations: the Australian Society of Accountants and the Institute of Chartered Accountants of Australia, and suggested a merger is likely. In addition, there is a third professional organisation for accountants, the National Institute of Accountants (NIA). The NIA and its predecessors have had strong links with the TAFE system and its accounting graduates. The ASA and ICA have related to higher education graduates. The NIA has a PD program (National Institute of Accountants, 1988). The NIA may not be acceptable to the other organisations as an equal partner. However, with changes in the tertiary education system and employment patterns (changes outside the control of all three organisations), new relations and tensions may be expected in the accounting occupation with its three professional associations.

While the employment status of the professions profiled ranges in varying proportions from private practice to the corporate and government sectors, teachers stand alone as employees in large state (or territory) departments or in the private or catholic systems.

One common characteristic of all the profiles is that the professions accept the importance and potential of CPE. Beneath the general acceptance, however, there are important issues as to what CPE is designed to achieve and how CPE programs should be delivered and assessed.

Policy and objectives

It was suggested in Chapter 3 that the question of mandatory versus voluntary CPE may have been a central, or the central, policy issue. The profiles have borne out that suggestion. A summary of the material presented in the profiles may be expressed in the following oversimplified form: professions have moved towards mandatory CPE as a single resolution solution to many of the problems facing the profession, with occupational therapists striving to maintain the voluntary principle and teachers unable to resolve more fundamental problems. The New South Wales solicitors and the ASA moved quite rapidly from what appeared to be unsuccessful voluntary CPE to the mandatory principle and the engineers seem to be caught in the same inexorable current. The decision in the former cases seems to have been taken without the clarification or even estimation of the full implications of what mandatory

CPE means in terms of other objectives or program delivery. In the case of the solicitors for example, the nature of what is to be acceptable content for CLE is being determined by a series of precedents of course approval, rather than the prior determination of objectives. The case of the engineers is somewhat different. They may decide for a minimum mandatory CPE but that policy is likely to be combined with other policies, such as the Career Action Plan, and further will be established within a professional structure that has traditionally witnessed members rising through the categories of membership.

The evidence of both the solicitors and the ASA indicates that the decision to instigate mandatory CPE, in terms of the timing and rationale, was made on the assumptions that the half-hearted attempts to involve members in voluntary CPE have failed (and were not likely to be successful) and that mandatory CPE would solve the problems of the public's and government's perceptions of the competence and integrity of their members. However, in so deciding, the professional associations overlooked other equally important policy issues relating not only to CPE, but to the profession as a whole. In deciding for the mandatory option, these organisations have merely deferred having to face these other issues. Can mandatory CPE guarantee anything to practitioners, the profession as a whole, other professions, government and clients? If CPE is mandatory, what limitations are placed on the role of CPE for the profession as a whole? In deciding for the mandatory option, these organisations have merely deferred having to face these other issues. What is the role of the association in the control of the content and delivery of the program, or is its role simply to approve activities and record compliance? Is there not the possibility that having developed a system, with x hours or y units of required CPE, that practitioners, good or bad, old or young, in private practice or the corporate sector, will learn, whatever else they are supposed to learn, to play the mandatory CPE game? What does the adoption of mandatory CPE imply about the meaning of education, its purpose and value?

Can mandatory CPE include the self-directed learning of the motivated professional and, if not, what will be the effects on those members of the profession who have consciously and conscientiously continued with their professional education beyond initial training? Is not the adoption of mandatory CPE a comment on the failure of initial training to develop an attitude of lifelong learning and professional ethics to its trainees?

SUMMARY AND EMERGING ISSUES 129

The evidence from the solicitors' and accountants' profiles indicates that there was not widespread debate within each profession about the drift towards mandatory CPE. There was some discussion but it appears in each case to have been narrowly focused and limited to the peculiar situation of each profession — with reference perhaps to that profession in North America — and not set within a wider context of, for example, lifelong education or the wider role of CPE. Further, the membership of the association, that is, those persons directly affected, do not appear to have been seriously canvassed as to their views, or needs.

The reasons for the decision to adopt mandatory CPE with its implied and explicit objectives suggest that Woll's (1984) warning about control is relevant. For example, if the power to license and re-license is linked to mandatory CPE, then the control of CPE means the control of the membership's freedom to practise.

The mandatory versus voluntary issue appears to be the major issue in CPE policy discussions in Australia. The evidence is that the adoption of mandatory CPE has been based on the assumption that voluntary CPE does not work and that mandatory CPE will solve that, and other problems. It is suggested, however, that although mandatory CPE may solve some immediate problems, it also raises as many issues and creates as many problems as it perhaps solves. Adoption of mandatory CPE appears to have limited the exploration of other important policy issues.

While it is accepted that the occupational therapists are a smaller profession than those discussed who have chosen the mandatory option, there are policy initiatives and practices evident in the occupational therapy profile that deserve consideration in other professions before the mandatory option is embraced. The CPE policy of occupational therapists appears to place a high priority on encouraging members to participate, not only in statements but also administratively — by the creation of interest groups. Persuasion and peer pressure to participate are viewed as longer-term methods for increasing participation. Further, it was noted that CPE has always been an integral part of the association's objective of promoting the profession and has been a high priority in the preservice training for the profession. The occupational therapy profile, in contrast with those of the solicitors and accountants, indicates an emphasis on longer-term policies to raise participation rates. Perhaps other professional associations should examine closely long-term policies before deciding on the mandatory option.

The over-concentration on the mandatory option has resulted in a lack of attention to other policy concerns. While there are policy statements, the emphasis on mandatory CPE has resulted in attention and energy being devoted to concerns about how compliance can be measured, rather than examining the overall program or noting changes in preservice training policies or changes in the higher education sector or changes in the composition of the profession's membership. Broader issues that were the focus of attention in Chapter 2, such as the dimensions of Houle's professionalisation (Houle, 1980), the orientations outlined by Scanlan (1985), or the implications of lifelong education or the potential impact of education as described by Gelpi (1985), do not appear to be taken into consideration, partly, it is suggested, because of the overemphasis on a narrowly defined discussion of the possible solutions to be provided by mandatory CPE.

Mandatory CPE, as may have been concluded from the discussion in Chapter 3 and here, is not generally favoured by the writer. However, mandatory CPE is a reality here and overseas. It is argued that mandatory CPE has been introduced for the wrong reasons and has had a negative impact on the discussion of other policy issues. Nevertheless, the author believes there may be a case for mandatory CPE in the short term in the large professions. A period of mandatory CPE may *force* members of a profession (particularly the 'laggards') to focus on the issue of CPE and all that it entails. At the same time the mandatory period would give the profession a 'breathing space' in which to examine the full potential of CPE, assess members' needs, and experiment with various methods of program delivery and evaluation. In this way CPE programs may become so pertinent to members' needs and so relevant to the context of professional practice in Australia that it will be unnecessary to make CPE mandatory in the longer term!

The potential for governments to influence CPE policy was noted in Chapters 2 and 3. With regard to the school teachers' profile, the major determinant of policy for their professional development has been the priorities of governments, both federal and state. In the reports of the discipline enquiries, mandatory CPE has not been strongly advocated. Encouragement rather than compulsion appears to be government policy. Mandatory CPE, as a policy advocated by some professional associations, may indicate more about professional associations' objectives of retaining elements of autonomy and self-regulation than a belief

SUMMARY AND EMERGING ISSUES 131

in CPE itself. Ironically, however, such advocacy for CPE does illustrate the potential role of CPE in a profession.

The profiles indicated that the role of state governments in the determination of CPE policy was not as yet highly significant, with the exception of school teachers. At the national level, discipline enquiries *may impact* on the professions under study and their CPE, and policies outside the Employment, Education and Training portfolio relating to the labour market, immigration, health and safety for example, *may pressurise* professions and their CPE, but the single most important effect the Federal Government can have on CPE is the White Paper on higher education (Dawkins, 1988). The changes created by the setting up of the national higher education system will certainly influence preservice training for professionals. More significant perhaps for CPE, however, is the section of the White Paper relating to adult and continuing education (Dawkins, 1988, pp. 68–70). This section, an important addition to the Green Paper (Dawkins, 1987), embraces the concept of lifelong education, suggested in this volume as a useful over-arching philosophy for CPE. Further, the distinctions between vocational and non-vocational education and credit and non-credit education are blurred. Also, higher education institutions are encouraged to become active in the field of CPE, on a cost-recovery basis. In addition to these significant statements relating to CPE policy and provision, the White Paper firmly places CPE within the general framework of adult and continuing education. The White Paper provides, therefore, a useful policy brief for CPE policy makers, who may be well advised to follow the way the statements in the Dawkins' White Paper become operationalised in the new national higher education system. (For a more detailed discussion of the White Paper see Brennan, 1988c.)

Management

The growing importance of CPE for the five professions discussed here is illustrated in the management structures being adopted. While the relevant national body has a role in terms of overall policy, the state (and territory) divisions of the organisations are concerned with the program delivery. Continuing professional education appears to be a central rather than a marginal activity in the associations.

The committees and the employees or volunteers who plan and deliver the programs appear to have been recognised as increasingly important, for example, those involved in CPE in accounting have been given more prestigious titles. A special agency has been set up in New South Wales to oversee Mandatory CLE, the compulsory CPE of solicitors.

An important aspect of the profiles in the management of the program is evident in the story of teachers. In complete contrast to other professions, teachers have very little involvement in the management of their professional development activities. While in the 1970s, there was supposed to be teacher involvement in PD management, recent developments have indicated that program priorities are determined by governments, both federal and state. With the numbers of Australian professionals employed by government agencies increasing, and with government policies regarding equal opportunity, multi-culturalism and health and safety becoming more significant for professionals, there is a danger that other professions may follow the teachers.

Program content and delivery

Analysis of the Profiles

The overwhelming evidence from the profiles is that there is no overall CPE program in the professions discussed. The lack of an overall program for CPE was evident in professions whether or not they have embraced mandatory CPE. Much activity was reported. New areas of interest for activities, for example ones beyond the narrowly technical or clinical, were identified. The use of distance education methods, computer-assisted learning, and even satellite communication for learning were noted as actual or proposed developments. Liaison with other professions, government departments, higher education institutions and the private sector was noted, supporting the evidence of the survey reported in Chapter 3. Special features, such as intensive activities or activities for those re-entering the profession, were recorded. As well as the use of new techniques and technology, the prevalence of the lecture/question session — reminiscent of preservice training — was also noted.

The sources of the program content appear from the profiles to be varied. For the occupational therapists the special interest groups were identified as the source of the ideas for activities. For teachers, content for activities seems to have become closely associated with current government priority programs at both the national and state levels. Ironically in those professions which have mandatory CPE, that is, CPE is regulated overall, the market place — an unregulated mechanism — largely decided the CPE program content. For example, the engineering profile indicated a change from provider-determined content to that of the market place.

In other profiles the importance of determining the needs of the profession's members was noted. The use of needs assessment instruments and practices was viewed as important (for data on needs and needs assessment see Brennan, 1988b; Cameron, 1988; McKillip, 1987). While the use of some form of needs assessment instrument is a general practice in adult/continuing education provision, there are problems involved in the practice. What sorts of needs are being assessed? How can needs be responded to effectively? Do practitioners really know their own CPE needs? How then is a balance between the needs of the individual practitioners and those of the association, the profession or society at large maintained?

There are also logistical problems. The easiest way to gain information on the needs of members is via mailed surveys. However, there is the possibility that another piece of paper requiring attention passing over the practitioner's desk may find its way into the rubbish bin or alternatively be given a quick response with the ideas of highest priority at that moment receiving a higher priority than may be warranted with reflection.

However, experience with a variety of approaches to gaining the needs assessment of members provides a possibility for providing, or having provided, a program that is at least based on members' views. Experience with needs assessment instruments also has an additional benefit in that those responsible for CPE in the association can gain a feeling for the concerns of members. The use of needs assessment instruments is not a one-off activity, because needs change. Seeking to gain an input from members with needs assessment strategies is, or should be, part of the on-going program delivery process. In some professions, the task of completing needs assessment surveys has been contracted out to tertiary institutions or consultants. This task, in the opinion of the writer, is not one that should be hired out. Not only is the information gained of importance to the CPE planners, but the process by which information is gained, is also important for the refining and development of the program delivery system.

The inclusion of a needs assessment phase in the development of CPE programs is likely to be beneficial, but as with the adoption of the mandatory option, there are problems with needs assessment and the problems of program delivery will not be totally solved by this one technique. Nor will an emphasis on the members' needs necessarily provide the basis for the overall program, as the needs of the association, profession, regulatory agencies together with changes in the social context require consideration as well.

In the profiles it was suggested that a basis for program development was the sorts of activities that had proven to be successful. What is being currently offered, both the successful and unsuccessful activities, can also provide the basis for generalising about the overall program. Rather than proceeding from clearly defined objectives, the objectives and goals can be teased out of the activities that are currently being conducted — by the association, tertiary institutions, and consultants. What evidence from the activities offered is there of the characteristics of professionalisation elaborated by Houle (1980)? From the activities of the program, what are the implied goals and which of the nine orientations proposed by Scanlan (1985) are being adopted? An examination of the activities provided allows for generalised comment on the goals of the existing program and for planning action to be taken to alter directions or stress other goals in future programs. The profile reports, for example, appear to report programs that focus on Scanlan's Orientation 1 (that is, updating/competency assurance) and perhaps 2 (that is, individual growth) with the implied goals relating to Orientations 7 and 8 (that is, systems deficit and systems improvement). As far as teachers are concerned the profile indicates that what seems to be desired and required is an emphasis on Orientation 3 (that is, professional reorientation).

Some Further Considerations

Todd (1987) has provided another approach for examining the program as it exists and for the provision of the on-going program. In his book entitled *Planning Continuing Professional Development* he describes three strategies (or categories of approach): profession-wide, organisation-based and practitioner-based. These three approaches are particularly valuable because they correspond with the three levels of goal orientation proposed by Scanlan.

In the first category, Todd includes the Practice Audit Model which has been developed in the United States, particularly through the Pennsylvania State University (Queeney, 1981; Queeney & Smutz, 1987), and has relevance to CPE planners because it is both a needs assessment and program development model. The model requires collaborative investigation between professional associations and higher education institutions to examine the practice of professionals. From this audit the CPE program is developed. The model has been adopted by a number of professions in North America.

In the second category, Todd's book includes a chapter by Ian Lewis on 'Teachers' School-Focused Action Research' (Lewis, 1987). This approach is significant because it highlights professional development in the workplace and stresses the on-going self-development of the teacher in the role of action researcher, developing as a result of action research his or her own professional practice. The value of action research in general and the role of the teacher as researcher has received much attention in Australia (see Carr and Kemmis, 1986). However, this particular approach to professional development appears not to have been widely adopted in other professions, either in Australia or overseas. In addition to any intrinsic value in action research itself, there is the concept of a 'new' role, that is, one of researcher, being used as the vehicle for the professional to develop his or her own professional expertise.

Todd's third category emphasises the individual professional practitioner. One chapter of Todd's book reports on 'The Use of Teacher Biographies in Professional Self-Development' (Woods & Sikes, 1987). If lifelong education is central to CPE, then a starting point can be the individual lives of the practitioners. Reviewing a professional career, whether short or long, can highlight the key points of a career, those tasks liked, those disliked, and what learning style the practitioner has developed.

The adoption of overall strategies for program management and delivery provide the CPE policy makers and deliverers with a framework in which to operationalise objectives. The strategies outlined above offer some options for the development and delivery of aspects of the program, for particular target groups, as well as providing data for short and longer-term planning.

The strategy of using individual biographies for the development of what the writers have called professional self-development, highlights an issue that was raised in the profiles. That was the degree to which the individual self-directed learning of professionals had been incorporated into the overall CPE program. In some instances, engineering and law for example, CPE in general did not accept such learning as part of the program.

Apart from the apparent injustice to those who may have developed their own particular, individual approach to up-dating knowledge and competence, the lack of recognition of the individual practitioner and his or her own learning therefore overlooks a large body of important research, not only on what professionals do in their own practice, but also research that has promise of being beneficial to the effective operation of CPE. Schon (1983) has stressed the value of what he has described as 'reflection-in-action' as part of the professional practice and professional development of a variety (but not all) practitioners. In a more recent book Schon further develops his ideas (Schon, 1987). Though concentrating on initial training rather than CPE (but therefore stressing the relationship between initial training and CPE noted in Chapter 2), he emphasises the reflective practicum. There is an easy translation of the reflective practicum of initial training into reflective practice in CPE. The emphasis on the individual professional's own reflection or reflection-in-action is important because it reinforces the concept of lifelong education since it values the individual and his/her learning as an integral part of CPE. Of relevance and importance in this context is the work of Boud and others on the relationship between reflection and learning (for example, Boud et al., 1985). To discount or dismiss the individual professional's learning activity or process is to rob CPE of a vital dimension and leave CPE open to the possibility of becoming an imposed and irrelevant set of educational chores.

The writer is at the moment developing an instrument, called Refpro, designed to incorporate some of the insights of the reflective practitioner, together with other characteristics, for use in professions as a means of ascertaining information on which parts of the CPE program can be established, monitored and evaluated. Other characteristics included are an emphasis on past, current and future practice; attention to various dimensions of professional practice; and evaluation of performance on the dimensions and consideration of how the individual would like to learn (or teach) about his/her weaknesses (strengths) (Brennan, 1988a).

Omitted from the professional profiles was an emphasis on the principles of adult education as a guide to program delivery in CPE. If there is to be effective teaching/learning in the program, then an understanding of key concepts in and approaches to adult education, for the practitioners are adult, may improve the effectiveness of program delivery. Merriam (1988) provides a brief introduction to the field. Jarvis (1987) presents a more comprehensive view with a specific orientation that may have particular relevance to CPE. Langenbach (1988) discusses 13 models used in adult education practice. The range of approaches, categorised according to purpose, include models directed towards vocational and competency-based training, self-directed learning and CPE. This literature provides varying models, with differing levels of sophistication, that offer the CPE provider guidance in developing an overall program for a particular profession. Finally, Holland (1988) has offered a model for what he calls the CPE 'process' that is not only descriptive but can test ideas and develop policies and processes, as well as plan, implement and evaluate CPE.

The profiles indicate that there is a need for an overall program for the profession's CPE activities. There are available techniques and strategies that facilitate the planning of an overall program to be achieved. The profiles indicated, as did survey data in Chapter 3, that activities in the CPE program involved a number of agencies. If the association is to be concerned for the program, apart from simply registering approved activities or the compliance of members, then some means need to be developed for incorporating activities provided by higher education institutions or the private sector into that program.

Evaluation

The profiles indicated that evaluation was not a high priority in the overall management of the CPE program. Financial accountability, for example in relation to the activities carried out by the special interest groups in the occupational therapy profession, appeared to be a major form of evaluation.

Where mandatory CPE had been adopted, the keeping of records may become an important means of noting general attendance figures for various types of activities. However, in those professions where there is mandatory CPE, perhaps the most important aspect to evaluate is whether individual practitioners' competence and integrity are maintained as a result of the CPE program that has been put in place.

In the development towards a more sophisticated and thorough form of program evaluation, it was noted in the accountancy profile that a movement towards outputs of the program, as opposed to the inputs (particularly financial), may be a useful step in the right direction. An instrument designed by Nelson, author of the solicitors' profile (Chapter 4), sought to measure the outcomes of the College of Law's Practical Legal Training Course. The detail of the instrument itself and the rationale on which it is based offer a useful basis for seeking to evaluate outcomes (Nelson, 1986).

It is not a question of whether or not the program, and the activities that make up the program, will be evaluated. Even if the association is little concerned with gaining data on the value of the CPE program, others certainly will be, and their judgements may not be systematic or objective. The participants will judge how valuable and relevant activities are from the point of view of their current stage of practice; other professions will judge the worth of the offerings of a particular profession, possibly in terms of the performance of its members in interdisciplinary teams or in disputes about boundaries. The reaction of governments, as employers and policy-makers, to this occupational group in the workforce may be determined as much by the perceived value of CPE as by official reports; clients may judge professional CPE either by abandoning the use of the professional service or having greater recourse to the courts.

Evaluation, preferably in relation of overall objectives (although also admitting the possibility of unanticipated consequences), should be carried out at the macro- and micro-level. At the micro-level in relation to each activity, those involved as participants, organisers and facilitators, should be able to comment on the activity so that the function of evaluation, improvement, can be facilitated. At the macro-level, the overall program and its impact should be able to be described, with supportive evidence to justify conclusions and claims of success or progress, or failure.

A useful overview of a variety of approaches that would be useful at both the macro- and micro-levels of evaluation in CPE is provided by Madaus, Scriven and Stufflebeam (1983). Another potentially useful tool

SUMMARY AND EMERGING ISSUES 139

for CPE programmers is the publication entitled *Standards for Evaluations of Educational Programs, Projects and Materials* (Joint Committee for Standards for Educational Evaluation, 1981). The four major standards — utility, feasibility, propriety and accuracy — offer a means of judging the value of evaluation techniques used.

As an integral part of CPE programming, evaluation procedures that provide information to the programmers, association and other interested parties at both the macro- and micro-levels regarding the inputs, processes and outputs of CPE need to be set in place.

Finance

The topic of finance could have been included with evaluation, partly, as noted above, because financial accountability appears to be the major evaluative element in CPE programming. In addition to this, however, is the relationship between the worth and value of the program and its on-going financing. If the program is to be based on the voluntary participation principle then the contents have to be 'valuable' to the practitioner in both the professional and financial senses. Where the mandatory principle has been adopted, the possibility exists in the short term that the element of compulsion may lead the market to demand prices higher than some practitioners can afford. In the longer term, however, such activities are likely to fail.

While the user-pays principle is widespread and while there were few recognised cases of activity costs proving a barrier to participation, there may be a need for those responsible for CPE to tackle the issue of finance for CPE in innovative ways. Perhaps approaches to financing other than the user-pays principle need to be explored. The engineers favour a beneficiary cost approach. The possibility of sponsorship for activities, as part of the process of raising the status of the profession as much as meeting program costs, may also prove fruitful. Cooper (1985) has examined some of the options for financing CPE in the legal profession.

In the profile on the accounting profession (Chapter 5), a figure in excess of $3 million was noted as the combined CPE revenues for the ASA and ICA in 1987. Professions would be surprised perhaps if accurate figures were obtained regarding the extent of their CPE expenditure. The importance of CPE nationally may well be enhanced if expenditure figures were able to be produced for clusters of professions or for the whole range of professions.

Closer examination of an individual profession's CPE financial transactions may also provide useful insights into two related questions: What sources of finance are being tapped for CPE, and in what proportions?; and Are the fees for CPE activities being paid by the individual practitioner, the strict user-pays principle, or are employers — government departments and private companies — supporting the participation of their professional employees in CPE activities? The 1988 survey, reported in Chapter 3, noted the impressions of CPE providers. Also the profiles present different answers to these questions.

The writer believes, however, that some practitioners — the young, the isolated and the married female members — may already be feeling financial difficulties in participating in the sorts of CPE activities that would be their first choice.

Because of the educational environment in which CPE operates, the importance of the use of cost–benefit techniques in the evaluation of CPE programs should be noted. The cost–benefit approach (see, for example, Thompson, 1980; Levin, 1983) provides a specific type of quantitative evaluation of an activity or program which may be used in terms of accountability and cost comparisons.

In both the areas of evaluation and finance, the evidence of the profiles is that while there may have been some progress in these fields in CPE provision, there remains scope for a good deal of further research and development.

Conclusions

Continuing professional education is an important and growing field in Australia. Such development may be expected because Australia, like North American and European countries, is in a period of social change when knowledge is expanding and technology is impacting on all aspects of working life. However, the particular characteristics of CPE in Australia are defined by the peculiar context in which professional practice operates in the federal structure. That is why attention was given in Chapter 2 to exploring the meaning of 'professional' in the Australian setting.

Part Two of this book consists of five professional profiles. They were chosen for specific reasons and are not necessarily representative. Caution is always advisable when drawing conclusions from small samples — in this case five professions of the very many that exist in Australia today. However, because the professional profiles were discussed within a predetermined 'framework' with elements that clearly describe *the most important issues* associated with CPE, some tentative generalisations can be made. We will now look at them.

First, there appears to be a lack of overall clarity in the purposes of the CPE programs of the professions. While there may be policy statements, the full potential of CPE has not been recognised. The possibilities have neither become integrated into the policies of the professions nor operationalised into their programs. In fact, programs as such are not in evidence. There is much activity, but the *overall purpose* of the activities has not been established. These omissions perhaps reflect the current stage of development of CPE in Australia and, in being recognised as omissions, point the way for the next stage of development.

Second, both assessment and evaluation of CPE programs and delivery systems appear to need more attention in terms of more appropriate strategies and techniques. If CPE is an important area of educational activity, and if professions are to benefit from the experience of other professions both in Australia and overseas, then the need for CPE research, and the dissemination of research already carried out, emerge as a major concern. Particularly important in the research and research dissemination question is the notion of cross-professional dialogue. Such dialogue can be assisted if higher education institutions, particularly those ones that focus on adult and continuing education rather than the initial preparation of professionals, focus on CPE as a field in itself, emphasising cross-professional contact.

The productivity of research is likely to be greater also if a cross-professional approach is used. For example, one area of current research activity in North America is the study of the appropriate mix of agencies for the planning and delivery of CPE programs (Belsheim, 1988). Another is concerned with the most appropriate locations for CPE activities (Cervero, Rottet & Dimmock, 1986). If research is carried out on such questions in the Australian setting, then, because these issues have relevance to all professions, the research should be *cross-professional* in preference to each profession carrying out its own independent study.

Third, the stage has been reached when those in the professions, as a group as well as in the professions singly, need to question the 'outputs' of CPE. With the apparent need to devote more attention to CPE program development, CPE is consuming a great deal of professionals' time and money. The attention so far has been on the 'inputs': the nature of CPE activities offered, the voluntary or mandatory issue, and so on. If there is one single area that should receive more attention, it is cross-professional debate and research on the *outputs*. Is it not time for professions to seriously examine whether all this CPE activity is having any impact? Is the mandatory policy making a profession more competent? Are all the activities creating a new confidence and accountability of members? If the professions do not undertake this task for themselves, then others, from other occupational groups, from governments, from the users of professionals' services, may make decisive comment and carry out appropriate action on their own evaluation of the outputs of CPE in Australia.

Not an 'afterthought'

As CPE continues to grow and flourish in Australia, the number of people involved in the field steadily increases. There are committee members who determine CPE policy and objectives. There are planners and facilitators of CPE programs. And there are numerous 'front-liners' who, either part- or full-time, are involved as lecturers, demonstrators or developers of CPE resource materials.

In the view of the writer, the time has come for the development of CPE programs specifically for the 'CPE-professionals'. It seems unreasonable — perhaps even irresponsible — to expect doctors, lawyers, accountants and other professionals to participate in CPE programs to maintain their competence, if the planners and providers of CPE do not themselves undergo CPE that will benefit their work. As indicated above, many CPE-professionals are essentially *teachers* of CPE: teachers are classified as professionals by ASCO and as such are candidates for CPE!

As with all other aspects of CPE, effective CPE programs for the CPE-professionals are most likely to eventuate if they are organised on a cross-professional basis. In conclusion, the author suggests that the quality of CPE in Australia will be a direct function of the rate at which CPE is developed for the CPE-professionals themselves. Herein lies a CPE field of top priority.

References

Belsheim, D. J. (1988). Environmental determinants for organising continuing professional education. *Adult Education Quarterly*, 38(2), 63–74.

Boud, D. et al. (eds). (1985). *Reflection: Turning experience into learning*. London: Kogan Page.

Brennan, B. (1987). Continuing professional education: Panacea, placebo or poison for the professions. Paper presented at 56th ANZAAS Conference, Palmerston North, New Zealand.

Brennan, B. (1988a). *Refpro: A needs assessment instrument*. Unpublished document. Armidale: University of New England, Department of Continuing Education.

Brennan, B. (1988b). *Needs and needs assessment in CPE*. Pre-conference discussion paper, CPE: Meeting the Needs of Practitioners, Armidale, September.

Brennan, B. (1988c). Adult and continuing education in higher education: The latest word. *The Australian Universities' Review*, 32(2), 39–41.

Cameron, C. (1988). Identifying learning needs: Six methods adult educators can use. *Lifelong Education*, 11(4), 25–28.

Carr, W. & Kemmis, S. (1986). *Becoming critical: Education, knowledge and action research*, rev. edn. Victoria: Deakin University.

Cervero, R. M., Rottet, S., & Dimmock, K. H. (1986). Analysing the effectiveness of continuing professional education at the workplace. *Adult Education Quarterly*, 36(2), 78–85.

Cooper, P. (1985). Continuing legal education — Who pays? *Australian Journal of Adult Education*, 25(2), 21–26.

Dawkins, J. S. (1987). *Higher education: A discussion paper*. ('Dawkins' Green Paper'). Canberra: Australian Government Publishing Service.

Dawkins, J. S. (1988). *Higher education: A policy statement*. ('Dawkins' White Paper'). Canberra: Australian Government Publishing Service.

Gelpi, E. (1985). *Lifelong education and international relations*. London: Croom Helm.

Holland, R. W. (1988). A theoretical framework for the process of CPE. In D. Dymock (ed.) *Continuing professional education — Policy and provision*, (pp. 36–48). Armidale: University of New England, Department of Continuing Education.

Houle, C. O. (1980). *Continuing learning in the professions*. San Francisco: Jossey-Bass.

Jarvis, P. (1987). *Adult learning in the social context*. London: Croom Helm.

Joint Committee on Standards for Educational Evaluation. (1981). *Standards for evaluations of educational programs, projects, and materials.* 1st edn. New York: McGraw-Hill.

Langenbach, M. (1988). *Curriculum models in adult education.* Malabar: Krieger.

Levin, H. M. (1983). *Cost effectiveness: A primer.* Newbury Park: Sage.

Lewis, I. (1987). Teachers' school-focused action research. In F. Todd (ed.), *Planning continuing professional development* (pp. 134–153). London: Croom Helm.

Madaus, G. F. et al. (eds). (1983). *Evaluation models.* Boston: Kluwer-Nijhoff.

Merriam, S. B. (1988). Finding your way through the maze: A guide to the literature on adult learning. *Lifelong Education,* 11(6), 4–7.

McKillip, J. (1987). *Needs assessment tools for human services and education.* Newbury Park: Sage.

National Institute of Accountants. (1988). *Counting House,* 4(2), June.

Nelson, J. W. (1986). *Review of the Practical Legal Course — Survey form (former students).* St Leonards: College of Law.

Queeney, D. S. (ed.). (1981). *The Practice Adult Model.* Pennsylvania: Pennsylvania State University CPE Development Project.

Queeney, D. S. & Smutz, W. D. (1987). Enhancing the Performance of Professionals: The Practice Audit Model. Unpublished Paper.

Scanlan, C. L. (1985). Practicing with purpose: Goals of continuing professional education. In R. M. Cervero, & C. L. Scanlan, (eds), *Problems and prospects in continuing professional education.* San Francisco: Jossey-Bass.

Schon, D. A. (1983). *The reflective practitioner: How professionals think in action.* New York: Basic Books.

Schon, D. A. (1987). *Educating the reflective practitioner — Towards a new design for teaching and learning in the professions.* San Francisco: Jossey-Bass.

Thompson, M. S. (1980). *Benefit-cost analysis for program evaluation.* Beverley Hills: Sage.

Todd, F. (ed.) (1987). *Planning continuing professional development.* London: Croom Helm.

Woll, B. (1984). The empty ideal: A critique of continuing learning in the professions by Cyril O. Houle. *Adult Education Quarterly,* 34(3), 167–177.

Woods, P., & Sikes, P. (1987). The use of teacher biographies in professional self-development. In F. Todd (ed.), *Planning continuing professional development* (pp. 161–180). London: Croom Helm.

Contributors

Barrie Brennan BA, DipEd(SU), MLitt, MA(UNE), MACE
Brennan is Acting Director of the Department of Continuing Education at the University of New England, where he is also a senior lecturer. His interest in continuing education developed while he was a secondary school teacher in rural New South Wales. He joined the University of New England's Continuing Education Department in Tamworth in 1973. His interest in continuing professional education developed from his experiences with school teachers and other rural professionals, and through teaching and research with students in the Department's diploma and masters degree courses. He has also played a leadership role in the national adult education organisation, the Australian Association of Adult Education, having served as an executive member and chairman. Brennan is currently the editor of the *Australian Journal of Adult Education*.

Glyn France MA(Oxon), MEd(Monash), DipT, DipCurrAdmin, MACE, MACEA
France is a professional development consultant to government and non-government schools in Victoria. His teaching and administrative experience includes six years as Principal of Ivanhoe Girls' Grammar School, five years as Principal of Gippsland Grammar School, and six years as Headmaster of Camberwell Grammar Junior School.

France has worked with all school systems in Victoria as a professional development officer, conducting numerous workshops on aspects of leadership and contributing to professional journals. He has researched the further learning attitudes of mid-career classroom teachers. In 1987 France established France Professional Development Services, and he currently provides a consultancy to the Ministry of Education and Western Metropolitan Region on professional development needs analysis and programs. He also provides direct support to schools and the teaching profession in areas such as teacher appraisal, time management and career development.

Gwynnyth Llewellyn DipOT, BA, MEd, DipContEd

Llewellyn is a senior lecturer in the School of Occupational Therapy at the Cumberland College of Health Sciences. She has had extensive experience in many areas of rehabilitation including services for people with physical, psychiatric and intellectual disabilities. For several years she held a consultancy position with the New South Wales Department of Education working with teachers, health professionals, parents and caregivers. In this position her interest in continuing education further developed, in particular in the provision of opportunities for a range of personnel in a variety of settings. Over the past three years she has also been involved in training programs for health and education workers in Thailand and the People's Republic of China.

Llewellyn was a founding member of a cross-professional organisation for physiotherapists, occupational therapists and speech pathologists working with people with developmental disabilities. Her current interests include the provision of adult education services for people with an intellectual disability and the continuing professional education programs required by therapists who are working with this group of people.

John Nelson BA, LLB(SU)

Nelson was admitted as a solicitor in New South Wales in 1971. After a period in private practice, he became a staff member of the College of Law in Sydney, where, for more than ten years, he was involved in the design and delivery of its continuing legal education (CLE) programs, as well as teaching in the College's pre-admission practical legal training course. Recently he has taken up a position as Professional Development Manager with Westgarth Middletons, a large national firm of solicitors. In this position his responsibilities include the design of his firm's training and education programs. He has been a persistent critic of the scheme of mandatory CLE for all practising solicitors in New South Wales and has published articles and spoken at conferences on the issues for mandatory CPE. His report of the major evaluation study he conducted on behalf of the College into its practical legal training course was published as a book in 1988. He is currently undertaking an honours masters degree in education at Macquarie University.

CONTRIBUTORS 147

Daljit Singh BCom(Otago), ACA(NZ), AASA, MAITD
Singh is the Director of National Professional Development at Touche Ross & Co., Chartered Accountants, which is a member firm of Touche Ross International. Prior to assuming his position with Touche Ross, he was a visiting staff member at the Department of Accounting and Financial Management at the University of New England, Armidale, New South Wales. His work experience includes lecturing in accounting at the School of Business, Capricornia Institute of Advanced Education, Rockhampton, Queensland. He has also held a part-time teaching position at the University of Otago, Dunedin, New Zealand while working for Coopers and Lybrand, Chartered Accountants, in their audit division.

Singh is a member of several professional bodies including the Australian Society of Accountants, the New Zealand Society of Accountants, the Accounting Association of Australia and New Zealand, the American Accounting Association and the Australian Institute of Training and Development. He has published papers on auditors' liability and his research interests include current issues in accounting, continuing professional education and training in professional firms.

Cyril Streatfield CEng, BScEng(London), ME(NSW), FIEAust, FIEE
Streatfield was born in the UK in 1928 and obtained his first degree in engineering as a part-time student at the Northampton Polytechnic in London whilst working in the Research Laboratories of Westinghouse Brake and Signal Co. Ltd. After further engineering experience with the British Electricity Authority, he taught physics at a London grammar school. He then held a short-service commission in the RAF, mainly as a lecturer at the RAF Technical College, Henlow. After leaving the RAF, he became a lecturer at the Northampton College of Advanced Technology, then he taught mathematics and physics for two years at Barker College in Sydney.

In 1960 Streatfield joined the staff of the Royal Military College, Duntroon and remained there for nearly 25 years during which time he was appointed Assistant Dean of the Faculty of Military Studies of the University of New South Wales and Head of the Department of Electrical Engineering of the Australian Defence Force Academy. Whilst in Canberra Streatfield gained his ME degree. In 1987 he joined the staff of the Institution of Engineers Australia where he is now Director, Education.

Australian Education Review

The Australian Education Review is a series of monographs on subjects of current significance and emerging importance to Australian education. Up to three issues are produced each year.

Offers of manuscripts are welcome. Reviews are usually no more than 100 pages in length and should be written for a general audience. All manuscripts are subjected to peer review before acceptance for publication. Further information on the requirements for manuscripts is available from Laurance Splitter, Editor, Australian Education Review, ACER, PO Box 210, Hawthorn, Victoria 3122.

This particular title was accepted for publication during the Editorship of Phillip McKenzie, Senior Research Officer, ACER.

Editorial Board

Neil Baumgart, General Manager, Schools Programs Branch, Ministry of Education, Victoria

Helen Hocking, Principal Education Officer, Education Department of Tasmania

Len King, Head, Educational Studies, Western Australian College of Advanced Education

Laurance Splitter (Editor), Research Officer, Australian Council for Educational Research